T0271555

THE NEUROSCIENCE OF

MANIFESTING

THE NEUROSCIENCE OF
MANIFESTING

The Magical Science of Getting the Life You Want

DR SABINA BRENNAN

First published in Great Britain in 2024 by Orion Spring,
an imprint of The Orion Publishing Group Ltd
Carmelite House, 50 Victoria Embankment
London EC4Y 0DZ

An Hachette UK Company

5 7 9 10 8 6 4

Copyright © Sabina Brennan 2024

The moral right of Sabina Brennan to be identified as the author of
this work has been asserted in accordance with the Copyright,
Designs and Patents Act of 1988.

Illustrations by dkbcreative

All rights reserved. No part of this publication may be reproduced, stored in
a retrieval system, or transmitted in any form or by any means, electronic,
mechanical, photocopying, recording, or otherwise, without the prior permission
of both the copyright owner and the above publisher of this book.

A CIP catalogue record for this book is
available from the British Library.

ISBN (Trade Paperback) 978 1 3987 1625 4
ISBN (eBook) 978 1 3987 1627 8
ISBN (Audio) 978 1 3987 1628 5

Typeset by carrdesignstudio.com

Printed and bound in Great Britain by Clays Ltd, Elcograf S.p.A.

MIX
Paper | Supporting
responsible forestry
FSC
www.fsc.org   FSC® C104740

www.orionbooks.co.uk

To Daisy
For your unconditional love

Contents

INTRODUCTION

Curiosity

Curious by Nature

Isn't the idea of manifesting alluring? Who doesn't want to make their dreams come true? I certainly feel the powerful pull of its promise. Beyond the very human desire to realise my dreams, I have a deep curiosity about how manifesting actually works in the brain. I became a psychologist and a neuroscientist out of a fascination with the brain and human behaviour. I am passionate, some say evangelical, about using neuroscience to help people understand how their brains work so that they can better understand themselves, improve their future and attain their true potential. In this mission I see many parallels with the practice of manifesting and notice that many manifesting authors, practitioners and influencers articulate similar goals to me. We all want to help people improve their lives, we just go about it in different ways. My approach in this book is to use neuroscience to explain how manifesting works and identify the manifestation techniques that are backed by solid science so that people can better understand themselves and manifest the future they desire.

Weeding out the Woo

Manifesting has frequently been written off by the scientific community as pseudoscience or 'woo'. However, on closer inspection a lot of the denigrating comments from scientists are directed at the misconception that manifesting is passive, wishful thinking rather than the active practice that is the subject matter of this book. By way of example, in 2021 the *Washington Post* published a piece entitled 'Covid brought "manifestation" back. But you can't simply will your way to a better life'. The gist of the article, which included comments from several mental-health professionals, is that manifestation is unscientific, magical thinking.

From the outset I want make it very clear that manifesting is not a passive process where you think your dreams into being – it requires action. Psychotherapist Dr Denise Fournier describes manifesting in pragmatic terms as the practice of transforming thought into reality by visualising your goal and then developing discipline to stay focused on and take action to achieve that goal. This description could be applied to many tried and trusted approaches implemented by people in respected professions (e.g. psychologists, psychotherapists, sports coaches, life coaches, personal trainers, etc.) to bring about positive change or achieve success. Why then is manifesting so readily dismissed as nonsense?

There are many plausible reasons. Firstly, it is possible that dissenters don't look beyond the headlines and so see manifesting as just wishful thinking rather than the focused discipline of taking action to attain goals. Secondly, there is sometimes a tendency for non-scientists to invoke quantum mechanics to explain manifestation. This often leads academics and scientists to dismiss manifesting as quackery because quantum mechanics is physics for tiny things and we humans – and the things we wish to manifest – are big things. Yes, it is true that humans, like everything else in the universe, are made up of atoms, and these atoms are composed of subatomic particles. However, on the scales we experience in everyday life, where countless particles interact, these quantum effects average out. We behave in a way consistent with classical mechanics because we are big and have lots of tiny interacting particles. Essentially, the weirdness of the quantum world doesn't persist at the level that we can experience.

Finally, there is the association of manifesting with magic and mysticism. My aim with this book is not to debunk the magical or the mystical elements of manifesting your desires, but to use neuroscience to provide another layer of understanding and appreciation of this amazing ability to manifest.

Neuroscientist Dr Alison Bernstein states in an article published in *Vice* magazine that manifesting is not supported by science, pointing out that we cannot conjure things out of thin air, nor can we break the laws of physics. Having said this, she goes on to clarify that she has no issue with certain aspects of manifesting, which she likens to cognitive behavioural therapy (CBT), such as learning to control our thinking, modifying how we respond to certain situations and developing new habits.

I agree with Bernstein, you can't magically make things happen, you can't defy physics. I agree with her about controlling our thinking and changing habits too. I also agree with Bernstein that some manifesting techniques are similar to those used in CBT, but where we differ is that this similarity sparks my curiosity and makes me want to delve deeper to understand what actually works and to weed out the woo, rather than dismiss the practice of manifesting as unscientific. In fact, recognising these commonalities is what makes me curious about the neuroscience of manifesting.

Cognitive behavioural therapy is about as far from woo as you can get. It is a well-researched, scientifically grounded type of psychotherapeutic treatment that helps individuals understand the thoughts and feelings that influence their behaviours. It is often used to treat a wide range of disorders, including phobias, addiction, depression and anxiety. CBT is generally short-term and focused on helping clients deal with a very specific problem.

CBT operates on the idea that our thoughts and perceptions directly influence our behaviour. Similarly, manifesting holds that, by consciously directing our thoughts and emotions, we can influence our actions and, consequently, the events in our lives. The goal with CBT is to help individuals develop coping strategies and healthier thought patterns that can improve their reactions to challenging situations. CBT aims to identify harmful thoughts, assess whether they are an accurate depiction of reality and, if they are not, employ strategies to challenge and overcome them. It is not difficult to see why Bernstein likens manifesting to CBT.

Scientific evidence supporting the effectiveness of CBT is really quite substantial. CBT has been shown to be effective for numerous mental health conditions, including depression, generalised anxiety disorder, panic disorder, social anxiety disorder, post-traumatic stress disorder and obsessive compulsive disorder. In the UK, highlighting its widespread recognition as an effective intervention, the National Institute for Health and Care Excellence (NICE) recommends CBT in the treatment guidelines for the treatment of mental health difficulties, including clinical depression and generalised anxiety disorder. CBT helps people to help themselves, and research suggests that treatment effects are durable. CBT has also consistently been found to be effective in more than 375 clinical trials for various issues – such as marital distress, anger, chronic pain, and many other health problems.

While researching this book I couldn't help but notice that many of the steps and techniques used in manifesting echo those used in CBT and other interventions used by clinical psychologists and many more accredited health professionals who deliver researched, respected and scientifically grounded therapies and programmes. Rather than dismiss manifesting as woo, my curiosity and scientific training spur me to take a closer look and resist the temptation to make a swift assessment. As you progress through this book, you will see that my deeper dive reveals the core components of manifesting, which relate to psychological theories and treatments like CBT that are supported by empirical evidence and can be explained by neuroscience. Manifesting works, just not necessarily for the reasons espoused by many manifesting authors, influencers, gurus and practitioners. Using cutting-edge neuroscience, this book explains how manifesting actually works.

Pretty much anyone can set up shop as a manifesting practitioner. There is no one method for manifesting. There is no governing body and no formal or accredited training either, much like the coaching and psychology professions. From a moral and ethical perspective, I find that problematic and that is why I have worked so hard to ensure my training as a psychologist is as rigorous as possible – I have obtained a first-class honours degree in psychology at the National University of Ireland, and while there I was awarded a Government of Ireland Scholarship to complete my PhD at the Institute of Neuroscience, at Ireland's premier university, Trinity College Dublin. These qualifications together with my research and my career qualify me for chartered membership of the Psychological Society of Ireland (PSI), the professional body of psychologists in my home country. As a consequence I have earned the privilege of adding the letters 'C.Psychol., PsSI.' after my name in addition to my PhD qualification. I will be using all of my knowledge and expertise to explore the practice of manifestation and together we will discover exactly why it works and how it can be productively and thoughtfully used in your own life.

Core Steps and Techniques

While misconceptions about manifesting abound and manifesting methods vary across practitioners and books, most adopt a step-by-step approach and use similar tools and techniques.

Once you read multiple manifesting books, as I have done while researching this book, you come to realise that irrespective of the number of steps or the types of techniques advocated by the author, when you peel away the magical explanations, mystical flourishes, the practitioner's personal world view, their trademark technique, their particular flavour of philosophy, religion or belief system, a common core of steps and techniques are revealed. In the chapters that follow I will explain, from a neuroscientific and psychological perspective, what happens in our brains when we adopt these core manifesting steps and techniques. This doesn't reduce the magic, but expands it, illustrating the remarkable, magical complexity of our own brains. Science doesn't necessarily remove magic from the world; instead, it often enhances it, showing us the intricate and beautiful mechanisms behind the phenomena we experience. The mystery may shift from the phenomenon itself to a deeper appreciation of the complexities of the universe and of our brains.

Storytelling

When the routine rhythm of our lives was dramatically disrupted by the pandemic, people began to think about rewriting or reinventing their lives. Many looked to the internet and social media for answers and found or, more accurately, rediscovered manifesting, which offered a means to a brighter, better future at a time when we all desperately needed to feel hopeful. Compelling stories of dreams coming true for ordinary people were the perfect antidote to the uncertainty and depressing nature of the pandemic and lockdown.

Storytelling is intrinsic to human nature. Whether it be our earliest ancestors' oral communication, the drawings in cave dwellings of 30,000 years ago, the hieroglyphics of Ancient Egypt, the written word, modern film, TV, photography, texting, or the social media of the internet age, humans have always relied on story-telling to learn, communicate and make sense of the world. We are social creatures. We crave connection. Stories are a powerful way to connect and to stimulate the brain.

Research indicates that a story is far more persuasive than information presented in straightforward factual form. Stories captivate us in ways that a list of facts just can't, because they are processed differently in the brain. When processing non-narrative content, the brain focuses on a series of facts and arguments; in contrast, to comprehend a story the brain must process information about characters, their intent, the sequence of events and so on. This results in a much more immersive experience that can activate emotional pathways in much the same way as they would be activated in response to real-life events. This deep emotional connection could be why we're often more convinced by stories than by the facts-only delivery associated with scientific content. We're also more likely to remember the information in a story than stand-alone facts, which, in turn, influences our attitudes and behaviour.

When we share a story with another person, we literally connect brains. The brain activity of the listener mirrors the brain activity of the teller with a few seconds' delay. This synchronised neural activity spreads beyond areas of the brain that process words to parts of the brain involved in understanding and meaning. The default mode network is a group of interconnected brain structures that activate together when our focus turns inwards – such as when we imagine stories, visualise, daydream, recall memories or think about ourselves. The stronger the level of synchronisation in the default mode network the better the understanding and the more successful the communication. Storytelling has been hugely influential in the success of manifesting.

Stories bring us together in a sort of collective sense-making that helps us to figure out the world and our emotions. Stories allow us to tie events together, consider causality and resolve ambiguity. Listening to stories told by others can help us to make sense of our own feelings and our personal situations. Stories can help us to regain control during challenging times. I think that this goes a long way towards explaining the surge of interest in manifesting that occurred during the pandemic.

Stories are powerful, and it seems that some stories are more powerful than others. Rather interestingly, our brains appear to be particularly good at remembering the kind of stories that are slightly out of the ordinary but not too 'out there'. One scientific study demonstrated this bias by testing people's memory for concepts that were a) intuitive (a grazing cow), b) mildly counterintuitive (a cursing frog), and c) extremely counterintuitive (a squealing, flowering brick). A week later participants in the study were most likely to remember the cursing frog! Stories that have some, but not too many, supernatural, magical or mystical elements, as can be the case with manifesting stories, are more likely to strike a chord and be remembered than either realistic or utterly unrealistic ones.

Stories are powerful, but not always in positive ways; they can easily be misused, as a very effective way to transmit misinformation and as a breeding ground for conspiracy theories. A compelling story, like a successful manifestation story told online, can draw us in and transport us in ways that make it difficult to consider other factors that contributed to the success. Captivating stories can also make it more difficult for us to spot lies and make us more likely to believe the skilled narrative techniques employed by those who promote propaganda, conspiracy theories and misinformation, knowingly or unknowingly. It's clear that this has contributed to the mountain of manifesting misinformation. My aim with this book is to provide a scientific resource to help you cut through this misinformation and focus your energy on what works.

Origins

Manifesting is more than a passing social-media trend. It is an ancient idea often attributed to Hinduism or Buddhism as both teach that our thoughts create reality. 'All that we are is the result of what we have thought' is attributed to Buddha himself. Helena Blavatsky, a controversial nineteenth-century 'guru' or 'phoney' – she has been referred to as both – is credited with popularising and spreading Eastern religious ideas and new-age philosophies in the Western world. Her book, *The Secret Doctrine*, which includes many teachings found in contemporary manifesting, draws on these ancient religions. Blavatsky emphasises our ability to sculpt our own reality and the role that our thinking plays in defining or limiting who we are and what we can do. In a meeting with a journalist in 1935, theoretical physicist Albert Einstein is purported to have said, 'Madame Blavatsky is a bit wild and somewhat irrational and speaks as if she were the Oracle of Delphi, but I will admit that I find some interesting observations in her book *The Secret Doctrine,* which was published in 1888, a time when physics and science were in their swaddling clothes. I'm astonished how much in keeping it is with modern physics.'

The practice of manifesting has since been popularised in the twentieth and twenty-first centuries by people like Deepak Chopra, Eckhart Tolle, Gabrielle Bernstein and Iyanla Vanzant. In 2006, the practice was the focus of the Rhonda Byrne film *The Secret* and her book of the same name, which sold 30 million copies. Thomas Troward, another influential figure from the nineteenth century, who combined teachings from various ancient spiritual traditions, is thought to have influenced *The Secret*.

The early twentieth century saw a proliferation of writing on the 'law of attraction' and the emergence of a trend to illustrate concepts and ideas with personal success stories – something that clearly contributes to the endurance and appeal of the idea. William Walker Atkinson, who wrote 100 books and edited the *New Thought* journal, drew heavily on Hindu philosophy. While I don't agree with everything he wrote, some of his ideas – such as 'We generally see that for which we look' – are supported by neuroscience. While Wallace D. Wattles, the author of *The Science of Getting Rich*, is overly dismissive of the negative impact of socio-economic differences, his book presents some clear practical advice and encourages creative visualisation, which is not only a cornerstone of contemporary manifestation but is also a technique frequently used effectively in therapeutic, clinical and holistic settings by psychologists, psychotherapists and performance coaches.

Science and Magic

In addition to personal success stories of manifesting, much of manifesting's allure comes from its mysterious, supernatural and magical associations. Manifesting your dreams is a magical experience. How things seem is not necessarily how they are. Understanding how things are will not necessarily change how things seem. On the surface, manifesting can seem like magic, but that doesn't mean that it is magic. Understanding the underlying science won't make the experience feel any less magical. Understanding the mechanics, the science, of how you manifested your ideal home, husband or career won't make the experience any less special. You will still have manifested your desires and it will still feel magical.

Our tendency to think of science as the antithesis of magic belies their intertwined history. What seems scientific to us now was magic to those living in the pre-modern period: thunderstorms, lightning and natural disasters were often attributed to magical forces or the anger of the gods; solar and lunar eclipses were seen as supernatural events; and comets were considered harbingers of doom. Historically, we have deemed that which we don't understand to be magic, sorcery or witchcraft. Mental disorders were associated with possession or witchcraft, and various plants and herbs used for medicinal purposes were often given mystical or magical healing powers. Professor Alec Ryrie, whose research interests include the historic relationship between science, magic and religion, proposes that 'science is basically magic that works'. Fundamentally, once we figure out how something mysterious works using the rigorous scientific method, that 'something' is no longer mysterious and as a consequence moves from the realm of magic to the domain of science. That, in essence, is what I aim to achieve with this book. I want to move the core aspects of manifesting – the aspects that genuinely work – from the realm of mystery and magic into the practical, awe-inspiring and, dare I say it, magical world of knowledge and solid science.

The scientific method is a set of procedures, guidelines and assumptions required for the systematic collection, interpretation and verification of data and the discovery of evidence that can be reliably reproduced, enabling scientific laws to be stated or modified. It involves formulating hypotheses and testing them to evaluate whether they hold up in the natural world. For example, if you wanted to test whether plants grow better with more sunlight, your hypothesis could be: 'If I expose one group of plants to more sunlight and another group to less sunlight, then the group with more sunlight will show healthier and faster growth'. When a hypothesis has been successfully proven it can lead to a scientific law (e.g. Newton's law of universal gravitation) or a scientific theory (e.g. the germ theory of disease). Hypotheses are proposed explanations for natural phenomena, which can be tested by carrying out scientific experiments designed to disprove them. Over time and multiple experiments scientists can eventually build enough evidence to support their hypothesis, at which point it can become a theory with power to predict.

The 'law of attraction', often associated with manifestation, cannot be classified as a scientific law because it does not come from rigorously tested hypotheses, experiments or observation. At the broadest level there are two flavours of manifesting: manifesting with the 'law of attraction' or manifesting without the 'law of attraction'. In its most extreme incarnation the former represents a world view where our thoughts and feelings vibrate, transmitting powerful messages that are received by a higher power (e.g. the universe, a higher self or god). The higher power then sends back life experiences that match the original thoughts and emotions. The manifesting explored in this book is the latter. It does not require belief in pseudoscience or spiritual or supernatural powers; instead it is founded on the idea that we can set ambitious goals, act in alignment with those goals and notice and capitalise on opportunities because manifesting practices prime us to pay attention to elements in our environment relevant to our goals.

While much of the scepticism surrounding manifesting is fuelled by pervasive misinformation and, in some cases, the misrepresentation of science, there is also a sort of scientific snobbery at play. It seems sophisticated to dismiss manifesting as woo. In fairness to fellow scientists who do dismiss it, there seems to be an impossible number of self-proclaimed manifesting experts who propagate misinformation on the internet – it is difficult not to be sceptical.

However, it is rather interesting to consider that in the sixteenth century, at the dawn of the scientific revolution, to be sceptical and disbelieving was considered self-limiting. A willingness to believe was considered sensible in order to progress in light of what was then new mathematics, new geography and new astronomy. Depending on the context, both belief and disbelief can be as stupid as each other. From a scientific perspective, it is not sensible to believe without scientific examination of the phenomenon in question. But what many fail to recognise is that disbelief without scientific examination can also be nonsensical. To children, the uninitiated and those who only skim the surface, what is scientific can feel like magic, until the science is revealed. My academic discipline of psychology teaches me to be sceptical and that has value. However, rather than dismiss 'manifesting' outright, as many scientists and other sceptics have done, I am keen not to throw the baby out with the bathwater, or to put it another way I don't want to throw out what works with the woo. In this book I focus on the aspects at the core of manifesting that work and can be explained scientifically.

Supernatural Bias

Biases in our thinking and inherent trait-like differences in key brain networks influence how each of us interact with manifesting content.

Brain bias

Brilliant as the human brain is, it is not brilliant enough to carry out the complex statistical analysis needed to tease apart the elaborate relationships that we encounter in our environment. Our tendency to see meaning in chance occurrences and to confuse correlation with causation leaves us vulnerable to making false connections that can, on the surface, seem quite plausible, attractive and, on occasion, even scientific. Social-media content on manifestation is littered with fallacious connections. Some invoke science in plausible but erroneous ways and others unnecessarily invoke magic when there is a simple scientific explanation.

I find it fascinating that scientific research shows that we are predisposed to believe in the supernatural, and I think some of the most recent success of manifesting can be attributed to this predisposition. During times of uncertainty when we feel that things are beyond our control, whether that be feeling overwhelmed due to personal circumstances, a global pandemic, a war, an economic downturn, a relationship in turmoil or a health scare, we are more likely to see signs and patterns in the chaotic world around us. Research participants who are primed to feel they have no control over a situation are more likely to see patterns in a random collection of dots compared to people who have not had their sense of control manipulated by researchers. You may have experienced something like this in real life, for example when waiting to hear back after a job interview. When you are in that limbo where you have no control over the decision, you might start 'reading into' minor details, like the tone of the email, or their choice of words, when they said they'll be in touch, or how long it's taking for them to respond. You might think these details form a pattern that indicates whether or not you got the job, even though they are likely random and not actually indicative of the outcome.

Our cognitive biases lead us to see the world as created for us, with intentional design by a supernatural someone (e.g. a deity) or something (e.g. the universe). The more supernatural aspects of manifesting tap into the fact that the human brain is biased towards a specific type of thinking that allows us to believe in a higher power and to believe that invisible entities are doing things. Without pre-exposure to the idea of a deity, children as young as three will naturally attribute supernatural powers to invisible beings. The Pew Research Center (a nonpartisan fact tank in the USA) examined American adults' acceptance of, or belief in: astrology, psychics, the spiritual energy of objects or reincarnation. Overall they found that 60 per cent believe in at least one.

Generally speaking, unconscious biases arrive from our brain's attempt to simplify information processing. Understanding our brain's biases is relevant to manifesting because they can influence our perception of the world and ourselves within it. They can also lead to distortions, and inaccurate, illogical and irrational thinking, judgements and behaviours that can scupper our manifesting plans. They can be difficult to eradicate, but being aware of supernatural bias and biases towards ourselves and others can help us to make more informed decisions about what we believe and why.

The human brain habitually uses past experiences and personal preferences to process information. This allows us to quickly manage the vast amounts of data we encounter every day. For the most part these shortcuts, known as heuristics, work efficiently. Unfortunately these unconscious habits can lead to flawed thinking and bias. These biases can result in misguided perceptions, beliefs and decisions. We are mostly blissfully unaware of these systematic blips in our thinking because they are unconscious. You may have heard of confirmation bias, which describes our tendency to value information that supports our existing ideas or beliefs; negativity bias, which refers to our tendency to unconsciously give more significance to negative events and experiences than to positive ones; and the self-serving bias, which alludes to our tendency to blame external forces for our failures or when bad things happen and credit ourselves for our successes or when good stuff comes our way. Consciously checking our thinking, beliefs and choices for bias can help us to change our behaviour in pursuit of our manifesting goals.

Brain traits

Inherent trait-like differences in key brain networks influence how we reason, think and make decisions, affecting how we engage with the manifesting content that we encounter. Would you describe yourself as someone who always trusts their gut or an overthinker? Both represent extremes in terms of how we reason and make decisions, and neither produce optimal results. According to research combining instinctive feelings with rational analysis is the best way to increase confidence in your choices, especially when you are prone to overthinking and when there is no obvious correct response.

The dual process theory of reasoning and decision-making suggests that we engage in two types of thinking: Type 1, which is fast, implicit, automatic and intuitive, and Type 2, which is slow, explicit, deliberate and analytical. These two processes are also referred to as System 1 and System 2, or by a variety of other more descriptive names including: impulsive versus reflective, intuition versus reasoning, experiential versus rational and heuristic versus systematic. Type 1 has great capacity and operates effortlessly using memory associations. In contrast, Type 2 relies on working memory, has limited capacity and requires a great deal of effort. In short, System 1 is about what 'feels' right, what our gut tells us, while System 2 is about what 'makes sense', what is logical. Sometimes our gut feelings can be spot on because they act on subtle cues and are influenced by past memories and experiences, but that is not always the case. Judgement errors occur when we rely on gut feeling without considering the evidence, i.e. System 1 generates a faulty intuition and System 2 fails to detect and correct. We make these kinds of errors all of the time. For example, if a pub quiz question asked which is more dangerous, flying or driving, we might instantly intuit (System 1) flying based on a quick association with memories of plane crashes. Failure to question this gut feeling by thinking analytically (System 2) about the total number of car accidents compared to the total number of airline accidents will result in an incorrect answer, which in the grand scheme of things is no big deal. However, in everyday life, particularly when it comes to making important decisions or when manifesting money, this kind of error can be hugely problematic. For example, making financial decisions based on gut feelings influenced by anecdotal stories of financial success because it 'feels right' without taking the time to analyse risk, odds, affordability etc. can leave people vulnerable to fraud and financial scams. Researchers have found that those who trust their gut are also more likely to believe in conspiracy theories and fake news.

A recent study that exclusively[1] looked at the psychology of the pseudoscientific and spiritual aspects of manifesting found an association between belief in those aspects and a) risky investments, a greater risk for bankruptcy and fraud victimisation and b) religious and non-religious spirituality. Psychological studies indicate that the thought processes of religious believers and non-believers tend to differ. Believers often rely on intuition and quick judgements (Type 1), while non-believers are more analytical and deliberate in their thinking (Type 2).

Recent neuroscientific research examining differences in the brain characteristics of believers and non-believers, using what is known as a neural trait approach, has revealed differences in core neural networks that support the findings from psychological research and dual-process theory. In essence, this means that those with religious beliefs and those without tend to think differently. People who follow a religion lean more towards gut feelings and quick conclusions, while non-believers tend to analyse things more deliberately. Studies that have found trait-like differences in key brain networks between believers and non-believers support the theory that religious and non-religious belief are underpinned by two different ways of thinking as well as different neuronal signature traits. Religious believers are characterised by neural resting networks associated with intuitive reasoning, while non-believers are characterised by neural resting networks associated with deliberate reasoning.

It's not unreasonable to suggest that these neural traits may also influence how individuals interact with manifesting content. For example, people who favour Type 1 intuitive thinking may be drawn

---

1 While the researchers acknowledged the vast body of scientific evidence for the efficacy of the more down-to-earth practical aspects of action-focused, goal-directed manifesting, they did not explore those aspects.

to the more mystical or supernatural aspects of manifesting and may be more likely to intuitively accept the less scientific aspects, possibly because they feel an emotional or spiritual connection with these aspects. In contrast, Type 2s who might actually like to manifest a better life may be put off by the illogical, unscientific woo associated with the practice. Ironically the core, effective aspects of manifesting that I identify in this book rely on clear, thoroughly reasoned (Type 2) action that often involves questioning and changing our more automatic, unconscious (Type 1) thinking, attitudes and actions. It is my hope that unveiling the neuroscience behind manifesting will make this life-changing practice more accessible to those who tend towards Type 2 and more effective for those who tend towards Type 1.

I am not prepared to write off an entire and possibly effective system of 'manifesting' because it relies on 'belief', invokes god, trusts in the universe or relies on untested, unscientific 'laws' presented as laws of nature. What I am prepared to do is look at the processes and practices advocated and examine whether neuroscience can offer natural rather than supernatural explanations as to why and how they work. Throughout this book I will make reference to many manifesting books and well-known manifesting practices and beliefs and offer up explanations from neuroscience. My aim is not to discredit; in fact I want to offer scientific support for any manifesting processes that work. After all, who doesn't want to live their best life or make their dreams come true?

Neuroscience

I am curious by nature and it is this natural tendency together with my expertise that has allowed me to curate cutting-edge neuroscience to show you how the power to manifest, to make good things happen, resides within us all, within our brains. I'm a huge fan of curiosity; it is the key that opens the door to insight, ideas and possibility.

The manifesting myths, misunderstandings and misconceptions that proliferate on the internet are not covered in this book. To do so would give them life and cause confusion. The aim of this book is to offer a practical, neuroscientific explanation of how manifesting works. I have no desire to deconstruct, contradict or critique explanations proffered by others. I hope that by offering an account of manifesting methods through neuroscience and psychology the 'how' of manifesting becomes less mysterious. I don't require blind trust or faith in supernatural powers, magic or good vibrations. Instead, I lift the mystical mantle of manifesting with a firm focus on the natural rather than the supernatural. I take you inside your brain, to explain how neural mechanisms that you use every day can be harnessed through clarity, action and focused attention to achieve change and manifest the life you long for. I explain how we create, shape and even distort our reality. I acknowledge that the playing field is not level and touch on some factors that may explain how the manifesting journey may not be the same for everyone, and why some people struggle to manifest. All the good intentions, affirmations and visualisations in the world can't stop life's curveballs, but harnessing knowledge from neuroscience can equip you with understanding as to how manifesting can help you to be resilient in the face of challenge, and enable you to live your best life, despite difficult circumstances. I have written *The Neuroscience of Manifesting* because the world needs to know that manifesting is not magic, it's science.

Treating yourself with **COMPASSION** (Chapter One) and building a **CONNECTION** (Chapter Two) with and understanding your true self are foundational. Manifesting is fundamentally about taking action to **CHANGE** (Chapter Three). In order to manifest your desires your brain requires **CLARITY** (Chapter Four) about what you want and **COHERENCE** (Chapter Five) between your vision and how you think, feel and act; only then can you truly **CREATE** (Chapter Six) your best life using tried and tested techniques.

Many manifesting advocates place power and trust in the universe, but after decades of studying and researching the brain and human behaviour I can confidently say that the power lies within you, not with some external source. More specifically, I know that it is the human brain that holds the power and magic behind manifesting; it holds something far greater than conscious awareness. Our conscious experience is only the tip of the iceberg. Our conscious experience is the equivalent of what a magician lets their audience see. For an audience member, the parts we don't see – the work done by the magician that we are unaware of, the illusions they create – this is the stuff that makes the magic. As we consciously experience the world and our life in it we are blissfully unaware of the non-conscious brain processes, the illusions your brain creates that make the magic. Even our conscious awareness is an illusion created by our brain. Our inherent tendency to see that which we don't understand as magic has led to a situation wherein we credit external magical forces with outcomes that are the result of the work carried out by non-conscious processes in our brains.

Magicians sign an oath never to reveal the secret of any illusion to a non-magician unless that person also swears to uphold the magician's oath. This is critical to the success of the profession for the reason I mentioned earlier: when magic is explained, it becomes science.

Thankfully, neuroscientists take no such oath and I am delighted in this book to explain that the magic behind manifesting is the work of the greatest master of illusion – the human brain. Scientists who research the neuroscience of magic describe what happens inside your brain as the greatest magic show on earth, and I am inclined to agree.

There is simply no need to invoke external or supernatural forces or abstract constructs when the power behind manifesting actually lies within the natural biological organ of the brain. Is that not simply awesome? For me, that is magical. Why abdicate power to an external force such as 'the universe' when the power lies within you?

PART ONE

LAYING FOUNDATIONS

CHAPTER ONE

Compassion

'It is possible to travel the whole world in search of one who is more worthy of compassion than oneself. No such person can be found'
Siddhartha Gautama (aka the Buddha)

Self-Love

Manifestation often involves several steps and techniques that focus on creating a vision of what you desire, fostering positive emotions and beliefs around that vision and then taking concrete action to make that vision a reality. There is so much manifesting information out there that it can seem confusing or even conflicting, but, once you listen closely, what at the outset seems like a cacophony of songs is really just variations on a tune, of which the most common notes are:

Clarity: the first step is to get clear on exactly what it is you desire. This could be anything from a specific goal, like a new job, to more abstract concepts, like happiness or contentment. The key is to get a clear definition of what you want, write it down and make it specific.

Visualisation: this technique involves spending time each day visualising your desire as if it is already achieved. Imagine the feelings, sights, sounds and other sensations associated with achieving your goal. This detailed visualisation may confirm your expectations and give you confidence in your choices. Alternatively, it may lead to the realisation that attaining the specific goals you have chosen may not actually bring the desired result. Visualisation may bring greater insight or clarity around what it is that you really want, and so you revisit step one until you get to the nub of what you really, really want.

Affirmations: positive statements or affirmations are techniques used to reinforce your confidence in your ability to achieve your desires through repetition. This often involves replacing negative thoughts with positive ones and eradicating limiting beliefs.

Action: achieving the change that you desire requires taking proactive steps, in other words engaging in goal-directed behaviour.

Alignment: attaining coherence by proactively ensuring that how you think, feel and act are aligned with your vision.

Gratitude: showing appreciation for what you already have and for the outcomes you're working towards. Gratitude can help maintain a positive attitude and open you up to more opportunities.

The concepts of self-compassion and self-love are often implicitly woven into the manifestation process. For example, rather than make it a step, Roxie Nafousi devotes an entire stand-alone section of her book *Manifest* to the topic of self-love, explaining that it is the foundation on which all other steps are built. In this chapter I explore what psychology and neuroscience have to say about self-compassion and self-love.

Manifestation involves recognising and accepting your current situation before envisioning a desired future. This acceptance forms the foundation for making positive changes. Positive affirmations often focus on loving yourself and recognising your own worth, which is essential for building the confidence you need to pursue and achieve your manifesting desires.

I offer myself the same compassion
I show to others

It's okay to treat myself with kindness

Making mistakes is how humans learn

I am not perfect nor do I need to be

Loving myself is not selfish

Fig. 1: Examples of positive affirmations

When I was growing up in Ireland, if someone said 'Jill loves herself' it was generally taken to mean that Jill has an inflated opinion of herself. 'Jack' could also be described as 'loving himself' if he had a big ego. Sometimes you could see that these derogatory comments came from a place of jealousy, but other times it felt justified, whether it was said about Jack or Jill; it reflected the thinking that they acted as if they felt superior to others or that they were somewhat delusional about their own looks or abilities.

It wasn't a very nice thing to say about anyone and you certainly never wanted someone to say that you loved yourself. For many people, myself included, learning to cultivate and practise self-love is fraught with conditioned thinking that it is somehow selfish, self-centred, egotistical or narcissistic. These negative associations could be a very Irish thing or they could be a thing of my generation, but if the proliferation of advice advocating self-love in the self-help sphere is anything to go by then I feel it is a safe bet to assume that self-love is a challenge for a lot of people, whether for the same reasons as me or for other reasons entirely.

The American Psychological Association offers two definitions of self-love, the second of which echoes my childhood understanding of the term.

Self-Love

n.

1. regard for and interest in one's own being or contentment
2. excessive self-regard, or a narcissistic attitude toward one's body, abilities, or personality

Self-Compassion

While the specifics of manifesting goals will differ from one individual to the next, at the most fundamental level we are all hoping to flourish and want to manifest happiness, contentment and emotional wellbeing. Self-compassion involves being kind to yourself, especially when facing obstacles or setbacks. Manifestation encourages this, recognising that it's okay to have ups and downs on the path towards achieving your desires.

Self-love, as a concept, can be tricky to define in scientific terms, but it's closely related to other psychological constructs, like self-compassion, that have been more thoroughly studied. In fact, self-compassion is often used as a proxy for self-love in the research literature. Dr Kristin Neff, one of the pioneering researchers in the field, highlights self-kindness (being gentle and understanding with ourselves rather than harshly critical) and mindfulness (holding our experience in balanced awareness rather than ignoring our pain or exaggerating it) as key components of self-compassion. There's a wealth of research demonstrating the benefits of self-compassion for psychological wellbeing, including reduced anxiety and depression and improved happiness and life satisfaction, which explains how it is a foundational element of how manifesting works.

Research in neuroscience also provides some insights into what happens in the brain when we engage in self-compassion. For example, a study found that self-compassion was associated with reduced activity in the amygdala, a part of the brain involved in fear and stress responses, suggesting that self-compassion may help to soothe these systems. Furthermore, practising loving-kindness meditation (aka metta meditation), a technique that involves generating feelings of warmth and care for yourself and others, has been found to activate brain areas involved in empathy and emotional processing. While loving-kindness meditation is not routinely recommended in manifesting circles, its affirmations (see fig. 2) are similar to many you will find being advocated by manifesting authors and coaches.

Loving-Kindness Meditation Affirmations

May I be protected and safe
May I be happy and at ease
May I be healthy and strong
May I care for myself/you wisely
May I be at peace

Fig. 2: Affirmations: loving-kindness meditation

Buddhism has always emphasised the importance of self-compassion. This Eastern idea of being kind to yourself isn't the same as the Western concept of self-esteem, which often involves comparing ourselves to others and making decisions about our own worth based on these comparisons. Nor should it be confused with self-centredness, self-obsession, lack of concern for others or prejudice. Self-compassion in the Buddhist sense means showing love and understanding to ourselves, staying balanced and non-judgemental about our thoughts and feelings and experiencing a sense of connection with all human beings. To put it another way it means being kind to yourself instead of judging yourself harshly, being present with your feelings rather than getting totally wrapped up in them and feeling connected to other people rather than feeling alone. Self-compassion means treating yourself the same way a caring person would treat someone else, wanting to ease your own pain, staying balanced and not focusing too much on any one thing and feeling a sense of connection with everyone else, sharing in the ups and downs of life. In order to be truly self-compassionate you need to achieve and combine all three aspects: self-kindness, mindfulness and social connection.

In the world of psychology, we often look at how two things might be related to establish the strength of the connection. For instance, how does our ability to be kind to ourselves (self-compassion) relate to feelings of sadness (depression) or joy (happiness)? We talk about these connections as either positive or negative. Imagine self-compassion as a light dimmer switch. If you turn up the dial (increasing self-compassion), the room gets brighter (happiness increases). That's a positive relationship because when one thing goes up, the other goes up also. On the flip side, turning up self-compassion makes the room less dark (depression decreases). This is a negative relationship because when self-compassion goes up, depression goes down. The two things are related but travelling on opposite trajectories.

And it's not just with feelings of sadness or joy. Imagine other feelings and behaviours as different rooms in a house. When you increase self-compassion, the rooms filled with worry (anxiety), repetitive negative thinking (rumination), unreasonable perfectionism, bad moods and avoidance of unwanted thoughts become less intense. This means that as self-compassion rises these things decrease. Meanwhile, turning up self-compassion brightens rooms filled with self-acceptance, self-esteem, determination, independence, optimism, good moods, competence, thoughtful wisdom, initiative, curiosity and, of course, happiness.

So, where does this 'self-compassion switch' come from? It comes from the human ability to feel empathy and compassion for others. Think of these as the electricity that powers up the self-compassion switch.

Self-Kindness

Manifesting promotes self-kindness in a variety of ways. Through the process of focusing on desired outcomes, positive feelings and personal growth, you can learn to nurture a kinder attitude toward yourself. Manifesting can lead to a deeper understanding and acceptance of yourself, including past mistakes. By embracing imperfections and forgiving yourself, you can foster a more compassionate and kinder relationship with yourself. Manifesting can be a tool for cultivating a positive outlook, and nurturing a compassionate relationship with yourself. In essence, by actively focusing on positive outcomes, and integrating practices that foster self-awareness and emotional wellbeing, you learn to promote self-kindness.

Self-compassion is a nurturing way to achieve contentment through unconditional kindness. The interesting thing about kindness in general is that it benefits both the giver and the receiver. Imagine this – when you do something nice for someone else, even a stranger, it's like your brain is throwing a party for you! When you show kindness, the pleasure and reward centres of your brain light up as if you're the one getting the gift, not the one giving it. And it doesn't stop there. Being kind helps your brain make more serotonin, which helps you to feel calm and happy. And the good news continues. Kindness also triggers release of the brain chemical oxytocin, also known as the 'love hormone'. This hormone is multi-talented – it lowers your blood pressure, raises your self-esteem and boosts optimism. It's like getting a free self-confidence injection every time you do a good deed. But there's more! Your body also releases endorphins when you show kindness. These are your body's natural painkillers, so being kind can literally make you feel less pain. It turns out that being kind to others isn't just good for them – it's like giving a wonderful gift to yourself too. It's a win–win!

Regrettably, self-compassion has acquired negative connotations in Western culture. Kindness directed towards yourself is often seen as indulging yourself or being selfish. When we make mistakes we berate ourselves and beat ourselves up, often in ways completely disproportionate to the error. Even when things happen that are beyond our control we rarely consider responding with self-kindness. Instead, we put on a brave face, soldier on and suffer in silence. Unfortunately, by being stoic in the face of struggle and suffering we are depriving ourselves of an opportunity to harness an important, in-built coping mechanism.

For example, when self-kindness is practised towards a painful memory, it allows for the softening of that pain. It also fosters the creation of a kind, compassionate and understanding inner dialogue, which leads to a very real sense of compassion for the self, making it a core component of self-compassion. Imagine you have a particularly thorny painful memory. Every time you approach it, it stings like the first time, causing you pain and discomfort. Research shows that self-kindness can change that. A bit like soaking that prickly rash of a memory in a warm, salving bath. It helps soften the sting, making it less painful to touch or remember.

But self-kindness is not just about softening the pain – it's about rewriting the story you tell yourself about the memory. Instead of a hurtful dialogue that pricks and stings, you start a new conversation. One that's filled with kindness, understanding and compassion. It's like having a heart to heart with yourself, inside your head. In this conversation, you start to feel a deep sense of compassion for yourself, just like a friend showing you love and support in a difficult time. That's the beauty of the soothing and self-supporting nature of self-kindness, which is fundamental to self-compassion. In other words, self-kindness isn't just about making bad memories less painful – it's about creating a whole new loving and supportive relationship with yourself. And that is an incredible self-care tool to have, another important means through which manifesting works.

The human brain is biased towards the negative. This too is an important survival mechanism. In prehistoric times, it was more important to remember and learn from dangerous or harmful situations (like encounters with predators or poisonous foods) to avoid repeating them in the future. Noticing something negative can save our lives or prevent us from sustaining injury. This is why our brain gives greater salience to the negatives than to the positives in our environment, experiences and social encounters. From a survival perspective it is more important to register a negative that might ultimately save our lives than to register a positive that might mean we simply notice something pleasant.

However, in our modern Western world this negative bias can sometimes do more harm than good. In a world where we're constantly bombarded with news and information, the negativity bias can lead us to focus excessively on the bad news and overlook the good, leading to increased levels of stress and anxiety and a skewed perception of the world and of ourselves. The negativity bias can contribute to depression and anxiety disorders, because of our tendency to dwell on negative experiences and emotions and our propensity not to see or remember positive ones.

The negativity bias can cause us to make decisions based on fear or avoidance of potential negative outcomes, rather than on a balanced assessment of all information. It can harm our relationships too, as we may focus more on a partner's faults or mistakes rather than their positive qualities or actions. And finally, of particular relevance to this chapter, it can lead us to develop a negatively skewed self-perception. As a consequence we underestimate our abilities and focus on our flaws, undermining self-esteem and self-confidence. This negative bias together with societal, cultural and other factors can lead us to become overly self-critical, noticing and giving greater weight to the negatives about ourselves. While it's impossible to completely eliminate the negativity bias, being aware of it can help us manage its impact on our lives.

One key strength of manifesting that authors and other practitioners tend to focus on in their work is the power of positive thinking in overcoming negativity bias. While each may approach the topic from different perspectives, there are some common threads in their advice. For example, Dr Joe Dispenza believes that by training our brains to overcome the negativity bias we can change our thought patterns and, as a result, our lives. In his book *Breaking the Habit of Being Yourself*, he explores how we can replace negative thought patterns with positive ones to manifest desired outcomes.

In Chapter Four, I explain how with clarity the brain can filter information in the world around us and focus our attention on the positive and the relevant. Wayne Dyer, in his book *Wishes Fulfilled*, discusses the importance of maintaining a positive attitude. He notes that overcoming the negativity bias is a crucial part of this process. In addition to encouraging conscious focus on positive thoughts and emotions, many manifestation authors suggest techniques like visualisation, affirmations and meditation as tools to shift our focus from negative to positive. The benefits and the neuroscience of these and other techniques are discussed in Chapter Six.

Self-kindness also involves accepting and forgiving your own mistakes and failings. In Neff's model the polar opposite of self-kindness is self-judgement. In her book *Self-Compassion* she argues that self-kindness is more than just stopping self-judgement. Neff even goes so far as to liken self-compassion to magic, because of its ability to transform pain and discomfort into happiness. She says that rather than condemn our 'foibles and failures' we must come to understand them and acknowledge self-criticism as self-harm. Neff describes self-criticism as a habit that can be changed, arguing that self-kindness is easier to attain than most of us believe.

Currently there is not a lot of neuroscience research on self-kindness, but there is considerable research on its polar opposite, self-judgement, and its brother, self-criticism. There is also neuro-scientific research on self-reassurance, which is seen as opposing self-criticism and so in this way is a close relative of self-kindness. Research indicates that being overly hard on ourselves (self-criticism) can ramp up negative emotions both in our brains and in how we report our feelings. Less is known about self-reassurance: the flip side of self-criticism. Self-reassurance is described as a style of relating to yourself that is compassionate. A bit like giving yourself a motivational pep-talk. As I mentioned in the introduction, I am curious by nature and so, in addition to reading multiple books, blogs and basically anything I could get my hands on about manifesting, I decided to sign up for some manifesting newsletters. The kind of messages that have been popping into my inbox since signing up definitely fall into the category of motivational pep-talks: 'A better future is within your grasp, take action now, great things lie ahead', 'Positive thoughts produce positive results', 'You have the power to create the life you want', 'Treat yourself with kindness, you are worthy'. More generally, I noticed a common theme promoting self-reassurance, self-compassion and self-kindness emerges across multiple manifesting websites, books, blogs, social media posts and interviews.

To learn more about self-reassurance, a group of researchers in the UK asked participants to reflect on things that had gone wrong in their lives, such as mistakes or setbacks, while having the activity in their brains recorded in a scanner. They were initially asked to be self-critical about these situations, then they were asked to switch to giving themselves reassurance about the same situations. What the researchers found was interesting: when people swapped self-criticism for self-reassurance, the brain areas linked to negative emotions weren't as active. Participants also reported that they didn't find the experience as intense when they reassured themselves compared to when they were self-critical. This research is important and suggests that one way manifesting might work is that practising self-reassurance can help reduce the emotional impact of negative events. This then is a useful tool to support people through times of challenge and change, and make it more likely that they attain their manifesting goals.

Another interesting fact that has emerged from research into self-reassurance is that it is linked with experiencing less shame and depression. This research suggests that self-reassurance is an adaptive process that helps to control our sense of social safeness where we can experience feelings of being safe around others, being accepted by others and connected to the social world. When neuroscientists examine regions in the brain associated with self-reassurance and self-criticism they find that they operate in different ways. This evidence comes from research using an MRI[i] scanner to look at brain functioning by tracking changes in blood flow to the brain; this is known as fMRI scanning. Participants were asked to imagine responding to a specific scenario (involving not getting a job) in a kind or critical way. Self-criticism (self-judgement) was linked to areas of the brain associated with error processing and problem-solving, while self-reassurance (self-kindness) was linked to areas of the brain related to positive self-talk and self-feelings as well as areas related to positive emotions and compassion. These associations are consistent with findings from research examining the self-conscious experiences of pride and joy and the experience of compassion for others.

Our capacity to care is innate. Our brains evolved to care. One way the mammalian care-giving system works is by triggering the release of the hormone oxytocin. Increased levels of oxytocin are associated with strong increases in feelings of trust, calm, generosity, safety and connectedness. Oxytocin promotes bonding and is released naturally when a mother breast-feeds and when parents interact with their children. Increased oxytocin levels are associated with reduced levels of fear and anxiety and have been shown to reduce blood pressure and stress-related cortisol levels. Research indicates that thoughts and emotions affect the body in the same way regardless of whether they are directed at ourselves or at others. This suggests that self-compassion could be a powerful way to trigger the release of oxytocin and reap the associated benefits.

In stark contrast to the calm, self-loving caress of self-kindness or self-reassurance, self-criticism can activate the stress response. A dash of stress can be a powerful ally, driving you towards manifesting goals and helping you to cope with daily hurdles. When handled adeptly, stress not only bolsters resilience during times of change, it also prepares you for life's curveballs. Although acute stress can sharpen memory, persistent, uncontrolled stress can hinder learning, harm memory and adversely affect your brain's size, structure and functioning. Manifesting requires clarity of thought, willingness to change and coherent thoughts, actions and feelings. Poorly managed chronic stress impairs our ability to think clearly, moving us from rational thoughts, reflective actions and aligned emotions to unthinking, reflexive, fear-driven responses and feelings. In addition, chronic stress disrupts sleep, compounding these effects, making it more difficult to attain change and more likely that we fall back into old unhelpful or unhealthy habits.

The stress response, or 'fight or flight' system, is a survival mechanism for handling threat. We need optimal levels of stress to manifest. Finding our own stress sweet spot puts us in prime position to take on challenges and take the action needed to attain our goals. We may find too much stress crippling and become stuck, or we might run away from the actions needed to attain our manifesting goals, or we may resist the change necessary for success. It's important to note that too little stress results in inaction and sets the stage for boredom and depression. In addition to the stress response being triggered by the kind of predator threat posed by the proverbial tiger in the jungle or mugger on the street, it can also be triggered by psychological stressors like self-criticism or self-loathing; psychosocial stressors such as relationship difficulties or lack of social support; psycho-spiritual stress, which is an umbrella term that incorporates things like a crisis of values or lack of meaning and purpose in life; and physical stressors like illness or pain (see examples in fig. 3). In the longer term, one of the side effects of poorly managed chronic stress can be a form of chronic freezing, experienced as being stuck, unable to move forward or make decisions as a consequence of being in a persistent state of high alert, stress-induced brain fog,[2] and aversion to change.

Criticism, including self-criticism, can feel like an attack, triggering the stress response. Constantly bullying, attacking and criticising yourself could become chronic. Self-criticism can be really harmful, leading to all sorts of mental health problems, from anxiety and depression to eating disorders. We tend to think it's just part of who we are, a trait; like our height or eye colour. But it's not a fundamental trait; our environment and experiences shape it. Self-criticism is influenced by family and cultural factors, including racial discrimination, emotional abuse, ageism and homophobia. The good news is, we can change it. However, turning the tables on self-criticism isn't just about squashing negative thoughts. It's about seeing it as a mental habit and changing the way we think. Habitual self-criticism does more damage than just the words we say to ourselves – it affects our mental health even more than we realise. I will discuss the neuroscience of habits in more detail in Chapter Five, but it is important to note now that just recognising this habit can be a big step forward. However, simple awareness or good intentions alone aren't enough to create a real shift. To give it your best shot you need some practical techniques to lessen self-judgement and foster more self-compassion.

---

2 In my book *Beating Brain Fog*, I write at length about the role of stress in brain fog.

PSYCHOLOGICAL

Emotional Anger, bereavement, fear, frustration, grief, resentment, sadness

Cognitive Anxiety, experiencing the world as unreal or distant or distorted, feeling detached from your self, feeling out of control, guilt, information overload, jealousy, panic attacks, self-criticism, self-loathing, shame, unworkable perfectionism, worry

Perceptual Attitudes, beliefs, roles, stories, world view

PSYCHOSOCIAL

Lack Lack of social support, lack of sufficient resources for survival

Relationships Difficulties with children, co-workers, employer, family, partner, spouse

Loss Of employment, finances, loved ones

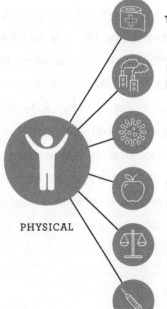

PHYSICAL

Trauma Infection, injury, surgery

Pollution Herbicides, inadequate light, noise, pesticides, radiation, toxins

Illness Bacterial, fungal, viral

Dietary Food allergy, nutritional deficiency, unhealthy eating habits

Imbalance Biochemical, hormonal, hypoglycaemia

Other Over-exertion, dehydration, dental issues, fatigue, musculoskeletal issues, poor oxygen supply, substance misuse

Fig. 3: Psychological, psychosocial and physical stressors

Mindfulness

Two handy science-based tools for this job are mindfulness meditation and loving-kindness meditation. These practices can seem challenging and removed from the goal of eradicating self-criticism, but over time they can steer your thoughts away from negative self-judgement. The goal isn't to stifle your thoughts, but to gently redirect your attention back to the breath without beating yourself up. When your thoughts wander, the advice is to just tell yourself, 'That's okay. Back to the breath.' Meditation, mindfulness and self-compassion affirmations are among the core techniques of manifesting, and yet another scientific way that manifesting works.

If meditation sounds like a big ask, Rachel Goldsmith Turow, author of The Self-Talk Workout, encourages people to try just one breath: 'Inhale, my friend; exhale, my friend.' She says that this one moment of non-judgement can be a powerful kick-starter to transform your mental habits, forging a kinder, more compassionate relationship with yourself. She says it's not about perfection; it's about progress, one breath at a time.

Mindfulness, a central pillar in manifesting and a potent spice in Neff's self-compassion stew, has its roots firmly planted in the rich soil of ancient Buddhist teachings, but over the ages it has blossomed into a more expansive concept, thanks to careful cultivation by modern psychologists. Consider how Brown and Ryan, authors of the Mindful Awareness Attention Scale, describe mindfulness: 'The state of being attentive to and aware of what is taking place in the present.' A beautifully concise definition that has been expanded upon by Neff, who sees mindfulness as a vital ingredient in the mix of self-compassion. According to Neff, mindfulness involves welcoming life's entire banquet, the tasty and the bitter alike. It's about acceptance, acknowledgement and understanding of our full life experience. Neff brings into focus the counterpoint to mindfulness, which she dubs 'over-identification'. This tendency to fixate, drown in or blow out of proportion our unpleasant experiences stands in stark contrast to the equilibrium that mindfulness seeks to cultivate.

So what does mindfulness really mean in practical terms? It's about lucidly observing and accepting what's happening right now, without judgement or bias. It's about bravely facing reality, no sugar-coating or exaggeration. Why? Because seeing things as they are – no more, no less – is the key to addressing our current situation in the most compassionate, and thus the most effective, way.

Imagine you're preparing for a big presentation at work. You've spent countless hours researching, crafting and rehearsing your pitch. The day comes, and while your presentation goes off without a hitch, exactly as you planned and rehearsed it, the feedback from your boss and colleagues isn't as glowing as you'd hoped. The immediate reaction for many of us would be self-criticism, maybe something along the lines of, 'My work just isn't up to par. Despite pouring my heart into this, it wasn't impressive enough. Maybe I'm just not as competent as I thought.'

However, if you take a mindfulness approach to this situation, you shift your perspective. You adopt a more balanced, non-judgemental outlook, considering both the positive and the negative aspects of the situation. 'Yes, my presentation didn't wow them as I'd hoped, and that's a bummer. I genuinely believed it would have a greater impact. But at the end of the day, I stood there, shared my ideas and I'm certain I managed to impart some useful information. Isn't that what it's really all about? So it wasn't a total loss, rather a learning experience. Now that I've acknowledged this, I feel more at ease and ready to focus on the here and now.'

With this attitude, you're not denying the disappointment, but you're not dwelling on it either. You recognise the positive elements as well, and this balance helps you stay grounded and present, ready to take on your next challenge. This means that this common manifesting tool works as a useful coping mechanism for negativity and self-denigration. Research shows that there is a direct link between mindfulness and general wellbeing, as well as lower levels of anxiety, neuroticism and depression.

Research doesn't just tell us that mindfulness feels good – it has also found that it can potentially create lasting neurological effects. Mindfulness has been conceptualised as having three interacting components:

Increased attentional control. This is a bit like upgrading your concentration from a dial-up connection to a high-speed broadband. You have the reins, and you decide where to direct your mental energy.

Enhanced emotional regulation. Think of this as becoming a conductor of your emotional orchestra, skilfully adjusting the tempo of your feelings. It's all about maintaining balance, never letting any rogue emotions dominate the performance.

Finally, mindfulness shifts our self-awareness. Rather than getting lost in a whirlpool of self-focused thoughts, mindfulness encourages us to tune in to our bodies, to feel more connected with our physical presence. It's like shifting from a 2D image of yourself to a more immersive, 3D perception. You become more in sync with the 'now' and the physical reality of being you.

The mindfulness advocated in manifesting helps you to cope with life's twists and turns, enabling a more focused, balanced and aware version of yourself! Let's look at the neuroscience for each component.

Attentional control through mindfulness

Researchers invited sixty-one people who had never meditated before to participate in a study to be carried out over a period of time. However, because life happens, twenty-three of them didn't complete the study. The remaining participants were divided into two groups: one group learned mindfulness meditation over a six-week course, and the other group took part in a shared reading course, which was designed to take the same amount of time and effort. Both groups reported doing practice at home. To see what impact these activities had on the brain, researchers took detailed brain scans of participants before and after their training. During the scan, participants completed a task designed to test their focus and ability to handle conflicting information.

For the mindfulness group, there was increased activity in parts of the brain (dorsolateral prefrontal cortex and rostral prefrontal cortex) that are key players in attention and decision-making tasks. There was also greater activity in several other areas associated with sensory processing and decision-making for the mindfulness group compared to the reading group. But that's not all. The mindfulness group showed improved performance on the task, indicating better conflict resolution skills compared to the reading group. So, in simple terms, after just six weeks of mindfulness training researchers observed performance improvements in parts of the brain associated with memory, focus and conflict resolution in people who were completely new to meditation.

Emotional regulation and mindfulness

The impact of mindfulness on our ability to manage our emotions is an intriguing area of research. One common approach to exploring this involves using brain imaging to see how mindfulness training might affect the parts of our brain that deal with emotional responses.

Researchers carried out a study with forty-six participants. They split them into two groups: one group got a quick lesson in mindfulness, while the other group were given a simple focus task. These participants then had their brain activity monitored while they were shown a series of pictures, some emotionally charged and others neutral.

The exciting part comes when looking at the results. In the mindfulness group, the area of the brain responsible for emotional responses (the right amygdala) was less active when looking at negative pictures. This decreased response was anticipated by an increased activity in several brain regions involved in managing emotional responses. In addition, when participants didn't know what type of picture was coming next, the results were similar. A broader look at the brain activity showed that negative images led to increased activity in certain areas but reduced activity in others, such as the hippocampus, which plays a role in memory. Overall these results suggest that, after just a brief lesson in mindfulness, participants' brains were better equipped to manage emotional reactions to negative images. It seems that simply being open and non-judgemental, paying full attention to the present moment, can help regulate our emotional responses. Isn't the human brain fascinating?

Researchers took a sub-group of thirty-six people from a long-term research project focused on compassion and attention and gave them training in one of three areas: mindful attention training, cognitive-based compassion training or an active control general health education programme. They all also had homework to do. The researchers used brain imaging to look at how their brains reacted while seeing positive, negative or neutral pictures, both three weeks before and three weeks after the eight-week training period.

What happened in the mindfulness group was fascinating. They found that the right amygdala, which as I just mentioned is typically associated with emotional responses, was less active for both positive and all types of images after the training. This suggests that, after practising mindfulness, the participants had a less intense emotional response to what they were seeing. Even more interesting is that this decreased emotional response was present even when the participants weren't actively practising mindfulness. This suggests that the benefits of mindfulness training might extend beyond the time you're actively practising it and could become a more usual part of how you experience the world.

Mindfulness and self-awareness

Many studies on mindfulness and self-awareness focus on a group of areas in the brain that run down the middle of the cortex (the crinkly outer layer of the brain). The default mode network includes these cortical midline structures, which are activated when we reflect on ourselves and our experiences (self-referential processing). Studies typically show that mindfulness meditation is associated with relatively reduced activity in the default mode network. By shifting activity away from brain areas involved in thinking about ourselves, mindfulness keeps distractions at bay, allowing us to focus on the present moment. The reduced activity in the default mode network during meditation has been associated with improved sustained attention.

One particular study explored this idea by differentiating between two types of self-focus: 'narrative self-focus', which connects self-awareness over time, the awareness that you have a continuous narrative or story, and 'experiential self-focus', which concerns immediate self-awareness or in-the-moment awareness of self. The researchers proposed that narrative self-focus reflects stream-of-consciousness, default mode network awareness, whereas experiential self-focus is the state of awareness that characterises mindfulness.

In the study, thirty-six participants underwent an eight-week mindfulness course. As part of the study, participants were asked to read different words while their brain activity was measured as they lay in an fMRI scanner. Depending on the instructions, participants reflected on these words either in relation to their own life story (narrative focus) or their current experience (experiential focus). Initially, when focusing on their life story, activity was seen in several cortical midline structures. However, after the mindfulness training, when the focus was on the present moment, brain activity showed changes. It decreased in cortical midline structures at the front and increased in areas associated with body awareness, particularly on the right side of the brain. These changes suggest that mindfulness can shift the brain's focus from self-narrative towards a more present, body-centred awareness. This aligns with the idea that mindfulness training, even short-term, can physically change the brain in ways that move us away from constant self-reflection and towards an immediate sense of our own existence in the here and now.

More generally, a critical review evaluated various experiments to understand how mindfulness changes our brain over time. They found that the practice of mindfulness appears to progress through several stages. For beginners, mindfulness increases activity in the front regions of the brain. These areas help control attention, directing it away from distracting thoughts and feelings and towards a calmness and composure of thoughts and emotions.

As practitioners get more experienced, this brain activity starts to decrease in the front areas, while activity in areas related to self and body awareness starts to rise. The connections between these areas also strengthen, helping to create a clear sense of self and body in the present moment. Eventually, with continued mindfulness practice, there's a further shift in brain activity. This whole process, from increasing focus on the present moment to a greater sense of interconnectedness, can be seen as a gradual shift from activity in the areas at the front of the brain to activity in rear areas. It continues to decrease in areas involved in self-reflection, while the sense of self starts to blend with the sense of others, creating an experience where the distinction between self and others becomes blurred, suggesting an increasing sense of interconnectedness.

Self-Acceptance

Self-acceptance may come naturally for those who received affirming messages from their parents and grew up in a supportive environment. When that has not been the case we must learn to independently affirm our worth. Manifesting can help us to do that, for example through the use of affirmations and positive self-talk. By consciously choosing to repeat positive statements like 'I am enough' or 'I am capable of achieving my dreams', you can build self-confidence and foster a kinder relationship with yourself. By concentrating on what you wish to achieve and acknowledging your unique abilities, you can recognise your potential and value. In essence, these manifesting practices and others including self-acceptance can help us to cultivate self-worth. Eliminating constant self-judgement, fostering personal fulfilment and becoming more compassionate and forgiving towards ourselves can help to foster self-acceptance.

Your level of self-acceptance dictates your happiness. The more self-acceptance you cultivate, the more happiness you will allow yourself to experience. To embrace a more loving attitude towards ourselves, the crucial first step towards self-acceptance, we must understand that our worth is not dependent on external validation. Engaging in approval-seeking often stems from our early need to prove ourselves to our caregivers, a relic of their conditional love. The realisation of our shared human experience, of a shared experience of unconditional love, can fuel self-compassion and can inspire a habit of kindness and goodwill towards ourselves and others.

Affirming that, despite negative self-beliefs, we have done our best can improve self-acceptance. Bringing self-compassion and understanding to each area of self-rejection can help lessen excessive guilt and shame, allowing us to better understand and forgive our past actions. Understanding the human brain can also help us to understand our past actions, making it easier to forgive ourselves and prevent repetition of past mistakes. In addition, developing self-acceptance requires acknowledgement that who we are and the choices that we have made have been shaped by our backgrounds, our life experiences and our biology.

More than anything else, developing self-acceptance demands nurturing self-compassion. It's only by understanding and forgiving ourselves for our perceived faults that we can establish a healthy relationship with ourselves. Which is a nice lead in to Chapter Two, which is all about connecting with and understanding your 'self'.

CHAPTER TWO

Connection

'Realise that everything connects to everything else'
Leonardo Da Vinci

Self-Connection

Connecting with your 'self' by gaining an understanding of how your brain and your experiences have shaped your sense of self and continue to shape your conscious experience of 'you' is foundational to the process of manifestation. Dr Tara Swart, author of *The Source*, says that aligning your goals and behaviour with your deep self primes you for success. Manifesting practices can serve as a pathway to discovering and embracing your authentic self. Gaining clarity through reflection and deep consideration of what you truly want in life increases the likelihood that you will connect with your personal passions and goals, rather than pandering to societal pressures or external influences. The process of gaining clarity about what you want to manifest requires you to focus on your personal desires, values and intentions, which encourage introspections and coherence with your core beliefs. As you strive to attain your manifesting goals, attaining coherence across your actions, thoughts and core values fosters authenticity and helps to ensure that you are living in accordance with what matters most to you. Manifesting techniques such as mindfulness and meditation promote present-moment awareness, which encourage you to tune in to your inner experiences and feelings, facilitating a deeper connection with your true self. Manifesting, therefore, can facilitate a deeper connection to what truly resonates with your core being, not only through introspection, coherence and mindfulness but also by encouraging self-compassion, creativity and self-acceptance. Manifesting harnesses creativity and self-expression through techniques like journaling and visualisation, which provide ways for you to explore and articulate your authentic self. The emphasis placed by manifesting on personal growth and transformation makes it more likely that you will evolve in ways that reflect your authentic self. As discussed in the previous chapter, manifesting fosters self-acceptance, which, in turn, fosters an authentic connection with yourself, without the need to conform to the expectations of others.

Without knowing yourself, how can you ensure that you will manifest a future that speaks to who you really are? It would be foolish to set sail without a compass. Charting a course towards a desired destination that resonates with who you really are is critical. You need to know who you are in order to know what you want. Otherwise you may find yourself adrift at sea or marooned on the rocks. Without direction you may find yourself manifesting someone else's desires or the life that you think you should manifest, rather than the one you really want. What you wish to manifest is inextricably linked with who you are and who you wish to become. The canvas of your future is in your brain. Every neural connection that you make brings you closer to the masterpiece that you wish to create. Manifesting encourages you to pick colours and patterns that reflect who you are and manifesting steps encourage you to do so with care and consideration to create who you aspire to become.

Self-connection has been described as having three components: 1) acceptance, 2) awareness and 3) alignment. In Chapter One we explored self-acceptance, and Chapter Five – 'Coherence' – focuses on the importance of aligning your thinking, feeling and behaviour with your true self and how, from a neuroscience perspective, this helps you to manifest your goals. This chapter explores what we can learn from neuroscience and psychology about self-awareness, our conscious experience of self, our sense of self, the 'me, myself and I' in our thinking, feeling and behaving as well as the role that memory plays in our personal narrative.

One of the key reasons that manifesting works is because it requires self-awareness, something that is essential to success in many aspects of life. Self-awareness is foundational to manifesting because it opens a window onto our authentic self, our core values and what really matters to us in life. Self-awareness is essential to our experience of the world. Self-awareness is an integral part of being human. Self-awareness allows us to question our decisions and choices; it also allows us to recall memories and question their accuracy. Self-awareness is critical for successful social interactions, allowing us to empathise, sympathise, display compassion and so much more. When I perceive my garden through my bedroom window my self-awareness allows me to reflect on how the morning light falls on the leaves and think how lovely the spring is. When I sit down to type at my laptop my self-awareness allows me to consider whether my vision feels unfocused and question whether it might be the sign of a migraine coming on. If you are curious about 'you', eager to understand yourself, or want to understand how manifesting might help you to build a better version of you, read on.

A great deal of the work that I do involves increasing people's awareness and understanding of how the human brain works and the role that it plays in who we are and everything that we do, feel and think. When we understand how our brains work, we understand how we work. Understanding how we work gives us insight into why we act and react the way that we do; why we make one choice over another; how our thinking, emotions and behaviour dynamically interact and influence each other. Understanding these things brings a level of practical self-awareness to people on the manifesting path, helping them to gain insight into what they really want from life as well as more focused, directional control over their thinking, emotions and behaviour so that they can maximise their potential. Manifesting, self-help and self-improvement require self-awareness.

If I were to give you my heart, physically via heart transplant not metaphorically, you would still be you. If you were to return the compliment and give me your heart, I would still be me but with your heart. If we were to swap brains, then who would we be? You would of course be you but in my body and I would be me inside your body. Your sense of self resides within your brain. Wherever your brain goes you go. You are your brain.

Your sense of self is constructed by billions of bits of information processed by your brain over the course of your life. The validity of that sense of self is totally contingent on the accuracy and relevance of the data available to and processed by your brain. Much of the data that your brain is using to construct your 'sense of self' is obsolete, untrue or irrelevant. Is this information limiting? Is it preventing you from knowing your authentic self, reaching your true potential and manifesting your best life?

Before you embark on your manifesting journey I encourage you to invest time interrogating the accuracy of the data with which your very sense of self is constructed. Your brain uses data from multiple sources collected across your lifespan to create what you experience as your 'self'. Most of this information, some of which goes back to early childhood, has been incorporated into your sense of self by your brain without any conscious examination of its accuracy or validity. Manifesting represents an opportunity for that to change, a stock-check, a catalyst propelling you to actively examine this data, trace it back to its origins and test its veracity.

Memory

Erik Pevernagie, artist and author of *Words of Wisdom*, says that we are what we remember, arguing that if we lose our memories we also lose access to our identity because our self-identity is the accumulation of our life experience.

Memory is a continuous mental process that plays an integral role in the construction of your sense of self. Your memories weave the story of you. You are an ongoing journey. You are where you have been. This story of you is embedded in the neural circuitry in your brain. This information informs your future self and shapes the choices that you make and the directions that you take. Does this mean that we are our memories? Does it mean that you know who you are because you remember where you have been? Are we really the sum-total of our memories? Are your memories reliable? Can you trust your own memory? I raise these questions not to get you questioning the integrity of all of your memories, but rather to make you aware that you can't always trust memories and that it is a worthwhile exercise to examine the validity of memories that are deeply woven into your personal narrative.

The perspective you have taken through a combination of conscious choice and unconscious processing is error prone because it is vulnerable to biases, heuristics and habitual thinking patterns. The story of you is not immutable; you can take a different perspective, rectify errors, shift your sense of self and rewrite your story. In a way this is what manifesting encourages you to do. This, I believe, is one of the liberating ideas at the core of manifesting. We have a tendency to take our sense of narrative self as fact. It's a good idea to check and update the story of you regularly, to question the origins and validity of anything that contributes to your sense of self, and your sense of self-worth, with a specific focus on limiting aspects that may hold you back from manifesting your best life.

Journalist and bestselling author of *Help Me!*, Marianne Power, spent twelve months on a journey through self-help books. In her second month Marianne followed the advice of Kate Northrup, author of *Money, A Love Story*. The insights that Marianne shared with me when I interviewed her are a good illustration of how we can allow our childhood interpretation of a single episode to majorly influence our behaviour, thinking and feelings as adults.

Marianne told me that money is a painful subject for her because she doesn't manage it well. She singled out a question from Northrup that she found particularly helpful: What is your first money memory? She recalled her dad, a builder, coming home from work with a bundle of cash. Marianne and her sister were watching TV and their dad threw the notes up in the air and told the girls that they could keep whatever they caught. Marianne recalls feeling stressed because she thought that she was going to mess up and that her taller sister would get all of the notes. She recalls great excitement and jumping and trying and then disappointment when after all of their efforts her dad said, 'Only joking, give it back.' Marianne is keen to make clear that her dad meant no harm and was generally generous. Nonetheless, she thinks that event had a far-reaching influence on her attitude towards and behaviour with money. She says she feels that 'money is to be thrown around. . . dispensed everywhere. I think you never get to keep it. So what's the point in looking after it?' Despite doing a lot of work on her relationship with money, these things run so deep that she thought that someone would come and take the advances she got for her super-successful book.

Whether you want to manifest money, a mansion, a Mercedes or a pair of Manolo Blahnik shoes, investigating the origins of your relationship to or perception of whatever it is you wish to manifest can reveal helpful insights for your manifesting journey. Awareness can change the trajectory of your manifesting adventure, but you will also need to take action to manifest lasting change.

Marianne went on to share the following anecdote:

> I always say that I'm not good with numbers, and that affects my relationship with money. I grew up believing I wasn't good at maths when I was at school, and then a while ago my mum was moving out of her flat and we were clearing things out. I was going through old school reports, and I found one that said how great I was at maths! Right then I realised this story that I had constructed somewhere along the way wasn't always true. I don't know if it's even true now. This was an a-ha moment for me. We limit ourselves with statements saying this is who I am, this is what I'm good at, what I'm not good at. And what I realised in the process of the self-help journey is that I am capable of so many more things than I ever imagined.

The self-examination and the questioning of your personal narrative encouraged in manifesting practices nurtures self-growth and provides opportunity for your brain to update the story of you in ways that more accurately reflect who you are. They encourage self-belief and positivity, making it more likely you will persist and attain your goals. Most of us carry around self-limiting beliefs for decades that could potentially represent the difference between manifesting and failing to manifest. Most manifesting step-wise programmes address this directly. For example, 'Clearing limiting beliefs' is Step 3 in Glyniss Trinder's Five Step Programme and Roxie Nafousi addresses it in the second step of her Seven Step Programme, Removing Fear and Doubt. She says that creating a vision board can give insight into fears and she urges readers to question the underlying limiting belief preventing them from adding something to their dreams and goals.

Self-awareness can be a powerful catalyst in effecting the change you desire. A journey of self-discovery can uncover many episodes from your life where your childhood self concocted a story to make sense of a situation you didn't really understand. Or you will remember an episode from your life that had a lasting effect on your sense of self or plays a central role in your story, your fears, doubts, insecurities or limiting beliefs only to discover on investigation that it didn't happen the way you remember or possibly even that it never happened at all!

Memory does not work like a recording device. As Professor Elizabeth Loftus, one of the world's leading memory researchers, says, 'Our memories are constructive. They're reconstructive. Memory works a little bit more like a Wikipedia page. You can go in there and change it, but so can other people.' I think Loftus's analogy works well as a way to explain how memory works in general. I want to stretch the Wikipedia analogy a little further in the context of the memories we reference to compile our narrative self. Wikipedia has a disclaimer that states it 'cannot guarantee the validity of the information found here... that is not to say that you will not find valuable and accurate information in Wikipedia; much of the time you will.' The same holds true for memory; much of the time it is a valuable and accurate source of information, but you cannot guarantee the validity of all of the memories that contribute to your narrative self. The content of Wikipedia articles is vulnerable to vandalism and can be changed or corrupted by someone whose opinion does not coincide with the state of knowledge presented. As you read on you will learn that memories too can be changed and are vulnerable to suggestion and corruption; you may even be holding on to memories that are simply the opinion of others and with a little delving discover that this opinion that you have assimilated as 'truth' is directly contradictory to the state of knowledge. This was the case with Marianne, whose memory of being bad at maths is contradicted by the evidence from her school report. While Wikipedia can be 'edited by anyone at any time', it has overt procedures in place to ensure the reliability, validity, verifiability and veracity of the content. Articles are fact-checked and all of the information on a Wikipedia page must be validated with citations from reliable sources. Some manifesting steps operate a bit like introducing overt procedures to ensure the reliability, validity, verifiability and veracity of the content of your memories and of the story of you.

Our memories are unreliable, but we generally fail to acknowledge this fact, especially when it comes to our personal narrative. Manifesting techniques can help you test the reliability of the memories that contribute to your own narrative before embarking on your manifesting expedition. My tuppence worth would be to carefully scrutinise the parts of your personal narrative that came from the 'opinion' of others.

Given that every atom in your body is replaced every seven years, your skin cells every few weeks and your red blood cells every four months, is there any part of 'you' that remains constant? Is there, deep down at the core, an unchanging self? We certainly experience a sort of constant self, but are you really the same 'you' that you were at five or at fifteen? Every experience we have shapes who we are, the changes are usually subtle, but can be dramatic if they occur after a traumatic or other life-changing event. Even injury and illness can change who we are. Our language alone tells us that: 'I feel like I've lost myself', 'I don't know who I am any more', 'You're not yourself', 'She was never the same again after the accident', 'Success changed him'. For the most part, the changes are imperceptible, but over time they accumulate so that the you at thirty is radically different from the you at fifteen.

Is memory the unchanging thing that sits at the core and gives you the sense of an unchanging, continuous self? As intuitive as that sounds, it is actually very unlikely because memory itself is not constant. Memory is an ongoing cycle of construction and reconstruction rather than a rigid static recording. The sights, sounds, smells, emotions of a particular experience, for example attending a friend's wedding, are each represented in different areas of the brain. Remembering your friend's wedding involves putting all those pieces back together. Sometimes a piece gets omitted, or an incorrect piece from a different memory is included during the reconstruction.

Consider a couple, Louise and Paul, who attended a spate of weddings last summer. When they share memories of the weddings with friends in the weeks that follow, sometimes the specific details get a bit muddled during reconstruction. Louise might remember Jane flirting outrageously with the barman at Katie's wedding and Peter might think that it happened at Susan's wedding. Both feel that they are right and the other is wrong. A scroll through photos on their phones proves them both wrong. Each time we retrieve a memory represents an opportunity to update it or modify it in some way. So, for example, when the friends get together and chat about the weddings they attended together Louise might subsume snippets from someone else's reminiscence of the day into her own memory so that next time she recalls the wedding her memory has been modified to include that snippet. Every time we use a memory it has to be reconstructed, and each time offers opportunities for errors and contamination from other memories and from the memories of others.

Memory is a biological process that begins with learning. Memory allows us to learn from past experience, guide our behaviour in the present and make predictions about the future. Learning is the first step in the memory-making process. Every new experience we have involves learning. When you learn someone's name or hear a new song for the first time, synapses between neurons are formed in your brain. These synapses create new circuits in between nerve cells. If you hear that song being played on the radio again and again the synapses will get stronger. Synapses get stronger or weaker depending on how often we are exposed to an event. Hear a song often enough and you'll eventually get to know the words. Chances are your memory for the chorus will be stronger partly because it repeats several times during each exposure to the song.

Remembering someone's name is much more difficult because in normal social situations you get one exposure to the name, on introduction, and frequently that's it. At the next encounter, social norms dictate that you should remember the person's name, but without repeated exposure to the name in the interim the synaptic connection is weak. Awkward as it may seem, repeating someone's name back to them after being introduced and using it several times during that first encounter actually works because the repetition strengthens the synaptic connection. Whatever flavour of manifesting you subscribe to, at the core there will be techniques such as journaling, affirmations and mantras that involve learning and also harness the power of repetition (see Chapter Six).

Memory influences how we act, think and feel with and without our conscious awareness. How and what we remember influences every aspect of our lives, our choices, our likes, our dislikes, our relationships, our world view, our identity and our sense of self. Understanding how your memory works is fundamental for understanding how you work. Memory is an incredibly well-researched topic, and as a result there are many ways of talking about it. Memory isn't a single thing or a single process, nor is it limited to one area of the brain. There are different types of memory. Most relevant to the discussion of the conscious self are episodic memory (recollection of events) and autobiographical memory (personal history, including episodic memories of events from your life as well as other facts about yourself, such as your place of birth, nationality, etc.). Episodic memory allows us to learn, store and retrieve information about specific personal experiences that occur in our lives, including information about the time and location of the event as well as details about the event itself.

Memories for episodes in our lives are not accurate reproductions of what took place. Memories are much more fragile than that. Everything you experience activates particular patterns of neural activity in your brain. Let's say you invite your friends over to see your newly decorated flat and watch a weepy movie together. A particular pattern of activity will be triggered by the small talk that you make as you greet your friends at the door. Another pattern will be triggered as they react to your paint-colour choices for each room. Likewise, when you settle down to watch *The Notebook* together.

When one of your friends reaches over to grab some tissues in preparation for the heartbreaking ending she accidentally knocks over her glass, and you look on in horror as the red wine spills all over your new cream carpet. The memorable detail of her spilling red wine on the carpet configures yet another pattern of neurons firing. All of these configurations become connected with a vast associative network of neurons that your hippocampus replays repeatedly until the associations become fixed. Neurons that fire together wire together, which means that stronger connections are established for neurons that are active together. The result is a unique pattern representing your memory of your friend's wine-spilling visit.

The strengthening of synapses isn't the whole story. Memory, attention, language, learning, reflexes, sleep, in fact all brain and nervous system functions arise from the activity of neural circuitry. Brain cells (neurons) communicate with each other and with the cells in the rest of your body via rapid synaptic transmission, which involves the release of neurotransmitters from neurons that act as chemical messengers, carrying messages across synapses.

Neuromodulators[3] are special brain chemicals that can influence how neurons communicate with each other, but in ways that are different to synaptic transmission. They have the ability to change how groups of brain cells work together, which can change our behaviour and how we react to different situations. This makes our brains very adaptable, allowing us to respond to new experiences and learn from them only at appropriate places and times rather than every single time an activity passes through the network. Being steered by relevance like this means that synaptic strengths

---

3 A neuromodulator is a chemical messenger released from a brain cell that influences the transmission of signals between neurons. Neurotransmitters are also chemical messengers released from neurons but they differ from neuromodulators because they carry a message across the synapse.

only change when something that is important to you happens: you see an advert for the dream job you are hoping to manifest, the details of the weather forecast when you are planning a barbeque or a Black Friday deal on that pair of shoes you've coveted for weeks. The network doesn't have to change when it encounters random, non-relevant information, so you don't have to register and remember every job advertisement, every weather forecast or every pair of shoes, just those that are relevant to you and your goals. This is why manifesting can be successful – it harnesses many tools and techniques that serve to improve clarity and focus, alerting your brain to what is important to you and to attaining your goals.

Our experiences become memories when they are relevant to our lives and especially so when they are connected to strong emotional states like happiness, fear, anger or trauma. Someone spilling red wine on your new carpet could have sufficient significance and emotional salience to become a memory. Nine months after the memorable wine-spilling a recommendation on Netflix for *The Notebook* triggers associations activating the specific configuration of neural activity from that night, taking you into your memory of your friend's visit. While you remember the event, you may not recall the specifics, for example, what you or your friend were wearing, what day it was, whether you had anything to eat and so on.

You'd be forgiven for thinking that your memory has faded because of the time that has elapsed, but it's not as simple as that. You don't have an endless supply of neurons. As a consequence, your brain cells have to do a double job. In fact, each neuron participates in different configurations at different times. Neurons behave dynamically and are under pressure to fire and wire together with other neurons in other neural configurations that represent other memories. Having the same neurons participating in multiple memory representations works well enough, but it means that some of the details can get lost or mixed up with other memories.

The interesting thing is that the memory doesn't feel faded or mixed up to you. We have a strong tendency to believe our own memories and to trust the memories of those who were present at an event. Encountering the research of Professor Elizabeth Loftus made me realise how much of what we assume about memory is incorrect. Loftus, a long-time researcher of human memory, is considered one of the most eminent psychologists of the twentieth century. Over decades of research she has demonstrated that memory, under certain circumstances, is not reliable. In fact, she describes it as malleable and easily manipulated. Her work has been crucial in legal cases, showing how witness testimonies can be influenced by suggestion or misinformation. Loftus's experiments show how leading questions or specific language can alter recollections. Her findings are relevant to manifesting because they highlight the fragility of memory and its potential influence on our personal narratives. For example, we may misremember a situation or have a memory modified by a suggestion that we assimilate as fact into our personal narrative of who we are and what we can achieve.

Alarmingly, her research shows how easy it is to get people to remember things that never actually happened. Volunteers were told about three real childhood events and one fabricated one, involving being lost in a mall. Twenty-five per cent of participants started to recall the fake event, even adding their own details over time. While this study, dubbed the 'lost in the mall' experiment, sparked controversy in relation to 'false' memories of childhood abuse, it has been replicated in other contexts with similar results. Controversy aside, the study underscores how malleable and error-prone our memories can be.

Rather interestingly, Loftus's research has shown that you can plant a false memory that ice cream, pastries or vodka made you vomit in the past, which reduces your real desire to consume them. They have also planted warm fuzzy memories of eating healthy food and found that people want to eat more of that food – asparagus in the case of this experiment. Although not consciously emulating Loftus's work, this is very similar to the approach I took to successfully quitting smoking. I told myself repeatedly that I hated cigarettes, that they were dirty, smelly things that I wanted nothing more to do with – and it worked. I haven't smoked a cigarette in more than twenty-five years. I'd had several failed attempts in the preceding years, including not smoking for a year. I believe my failure prior to adopting this approach was because I constantly spoke and thought about how much I missed cigarettes, how hard it was to give up smoking and how much I loved smoking. By simply changing my internal dialogue about my feelings towards smoking I made what had been an extremely difficult challenge into something relatively easy to achieve.

Memory plays a complex role in shaping our self-concept and belief systems, which in turn influence the process of manifestation. Given the malleability of memory, as well as its susceptibility to external influences and distortions, it's crucial to be aware of this when setting out on a manifesting journey. Manifestation requires coherence, which is based on aligning your thoughts and feelings with the reality you desire. Memories, whether accurate or not, form the basis of our belief systems and influence our perception of reality. As such, they can either support or hinder your manifestation efforts. Positive memories can serve as a powerful source of motivation and self-belief, while negative or distorted memories can lead to limiting beliefs.

If you remember instances of failure or criticism, you may start to believe that you are not capable or deserving of success. These limiting beliefs can become significant barriers in your manifestation journey, hindering progress and preventing you from aligning your thoughts and feelings with your desired outcomes.

Since memories can be unreliable and potentially distorted, it's important to critically evaluate any limiting beliefs that might be a barrier to progress. Self-reflection, meditation and techniques such as cognitive behavioural therapy (CBT) can be helpful in identifying and challenging these beliefs. You might find that many of your limiting beliefs are based on misinterpretations or inaccuracies, and confronting these can open the way for more positive beliefs and successful manifestation. Recognising the unreliability of memory allows for the possibility of redefining your self-concept and belief system. By consciously choosing to focus on positive experiences and learning from negative ones, you can reframe your memories and beliefs in a way that supports your manifestation goals. Visualisation, affirmations (Chapter Six) and maintaining a state of flow (Chapter Four) can also help to create a mental environment conducive to manifesting your desires. Memory, despite its potential unreliability, is a fundamental part of our self-perception and belief system. Being aware of its limitations and possible distortions allows us to challenge and overcome limiting beliefs, thereby facilitating a more effective manifesting journey.

Self-Build

Your experience of 'you' feels fixed, unified and continuous, something that just is. But the truth is that genetic, developmental, cultural, societal, personal and other factors and experiences contribute to and influence your brain's construction of you. We are often blind to this kind of change because it occurs so gradually over a long period of time. Your brain is constantly changing and so too is your sense of self. We are generally blind to the changes in our self. It's easier to see the change by comparing yourself now to yourself twenty years ago, or yourself in your teens or yourself as a young child. We tend to experience our 'self' as continuous, persisting from one minute to the next. Compared to our perceptual experiences of the world outside of us, our self-experiences are incredibly stable. This means that we often fail to register the progress we have made.

Manifesting techniques like journaling or even vision boards can support successful attainment of goals because, for example, you can revisit journal entries to register how far you have come and how much you have changed and achieved. While we tend to think of vision boards as future-oriented, as you progress through your manifesting journey they can serve as a reminder of how much you have changed and attained.

Your sense of 'self' is not immutable. It can change, you can change. Depending on the factors involved some changes will be more challenging than others so it is always important to remember that, despite certain unconscious biases favouring the status quo, the human brain is actually built for change, it is adaptive and resilient in the face of change. But change requires effort and it isn't always easy, although it can be. More about change in Chapter Three.

Ryuu Shinohara says that one of the reasons people fail to manifest is that they miss out on some fundamental steps. He says that you must create consciously. Before you design your future, you must first fundamentally 'design' the self that you wish to be and if you work from there you will inadvertently shape your environment.

Imagine you are planning to renovate or upgrade your home. You have lots of ideas about what you would like to do, you fancy something more open plan and you'd also like to add an en-suite to the master bedroom. You can't just jump in and start knocking down walls and adding showers and toilets willy-nilly without first understanding some basics about how your house is constructed. Well, I guess you could, but it wouldn't be wise because knocking down a load-bearing wall could bring the house tumbling down. Much as you might like an en-suite in your bedroom, it simply might not be possible if there is no access to a waste pipe or water supply. When you renovate, there will be things that you can discard, things that you can replace, things that you can modify and things that you may have to accept and learn to live with or work around. The same can be said for designing a new you.

If you are building an extension or planning to knock down and rebuild, you will need to invest time getting the groundworks right and ensuring that the foundations are sound. Unstable foundations lead to serious problems like cracks in the walls, sloping floors, malfunctioning windows and doors, damp, flooding, rot and mould. Correcting foundational problems after the renovation would be both difficult and costly. It is super important to have clarity about what you want from your dream home and how you plan to live in it. Envisaging how much better it will work, look and feel is, in a way, the easy part. However, if you focus only on the house from the ground up and fail to do the groundwork beneath, or build on faulty foundations, your dreams may disintegrate at who knows what cost.

Manifesting is a bit like renovating. Consider this chapter 'Renovation 101' for understanding how you were built, laying solid foundations for a new self-build, self-renovation or self-improvement.

In the construction industry it is considered good practice and is often a legal requirement to perform a ground investigation of the site to help identify how the site was used in the past and to determine stability and identify potential problems. The kind of self-investigation advocated in manifesting will go a long way in helping you to identify and address any potential issues before you start planning your manifesting journey. Groundworks investigations yield data that not only inform renovation or building design but also identify any areas that need to be improved, adapted or modified. Investigating the 'self' will also yield information about your self that you can use to inform your manifesting plan and ensure that it and your thinking, emotions and behaviour are aligned with your true self. And just as is the case with renovating a home, there will be things about your self that you can discard, things that you can replace, things that you can modify and things that you may have to accept and learn to live with or establish strategies to work around.

Neuroscientist Anil Seth says that self-perception is about self-control rather than about self-knowledge. The self-awareness espoused in manifesting practices connects you with your preferences and abilities and gives insight into and greater control over how you think, feel and act. Groundworks usually involve clearing the site, removing top soil from the footprint of the house. How deep the digging needs to go depends on the lay of the land; a sloping site might need to be levelled, retaining walls may need to be constructed. By now you get where I am going with this analogy: manifesting groundworks may involve some clearing out of patterns of thinking, feeling and behaving that have the potential to be slippery slopes back to old, unhelpful, unhealthy ways, such as negative self-talk, procrastination, avoidance or people-pleasing. Your manifesting journey will include setbacks and challenges; if you engage in negative self-talk such as, 'I always mess things up', or, 'I'm not good enough', it can reinforce self-doubt and erode your confidence in your ability to manifest your dreams, leading you back to old patterns of self-sabotage. If you frequently put off important tasks or responsibilities, it can create a cycle of stress, missed deadlines and subpar results. This pattern of procrastination can easily lead you back to old habits of last-minute scrambling and underperformance, making it more difficult for you to manifest your goals. Manifesting is predicated on change (Chapter Three), which can feel uncomfortable. Avoiding situations or activities that make you uncomfortable or anxious might provide temporary relief. However, this avoidance can reinforce fear and anxiety, making it increasingly difficult to confront and overcome those challenges, and ultimately push you back into old patterns of avoidance, which will stall progress on your manifesting journey. Constantly seeking approval and prioritising others' needs over your own can lead to burnout, resentment and a loss of personal boundaries. This pattern of people-pleasing can bring you back to old habits of neglecting your own wellbeing and neglecting your own needs, which are fundamental to manifesting. By recognising and addressing these patterns, you can break free from their grip and cultivate healthier, more positive patterns in your life that will take you closer to your goals. How deep you may need to dig will depend on how self-aware you are now, how much self-knowledge you have accumulated, how much 'self' work you have already done and how well you truly know and understand yourself. If you want to change your life you need to know yourself. Self-knowledge creates a powerful foundation on which to build your new life and your manifesting dreams.

Life is not a level playing field. If you and I begin a manifesting journey at the same time, on the same day, it does not follow that our journeys will progress at the same rate, in the same way because we are not the same at the outset. One of the problems with one-size-fits-all manifesting advice is the fact that one size does not fit all when it comes to manifesting. Critics have rightly pointed out that many manifesting advocates ignore or at the very least underestimate the

impact of systemic barriers. Issues such as racism, gender discrimination, socio-economic inequality will make manifesting more
difficult for those affected – not impossible, but definitely more
challenging. Oprah Winfrey, probably the most famous advocate
of manifesting, was born into poverty in rural Mississippi, where
she faced numerous hardships, including racial discrimination and
personal trauma. Despite these challenges, she rose to become
one of the most influential women in the world. But her story and
others like hers don't take away from the fact that the ability to
manifest is often easier for those in privileged positions, who might
have more access to resources or face fewer systemic barriers. It
is inspiring to know that numerous individuals have overcome these
kind of obstacles and achieved their dreams. Having said that, it
important to note that, while these people used positive thinking,
goal setting and other tools associated with manifesting, their
success was also the result of immense effort, perseverance, resilience and often collective action or societal change. Manifesting's
focus on the power of the individual can be a positive force but
also could inadvertently discourage societal efforts towards the
systemic change needed to address racism, discrimination and
inequality. There is a fine balance between empowerment and
blaming people for circumstances such as illness and poverty that
needs to be explicitly addressed in manifesting discourse.

There are many other differences between you and me
that will influence our manifesting journeys. Differences in our
predispositions will, for example, influence our ability to defer
short-term reward in the service of longer-term goals. Exposure
to early life stressors during critical periods of brain development
can, for example, heighten negativity and reduce positivity.
The important take-home is that actions critical for effective
manifesting like thinking positively and focusing on long-term

goals are easier for some people than for others. For this reason it is important not to compare the progress you are making on your manifesting journey with the progress made by someone else. The only meaningful way that you can measure your progress is by comparing where you are now with where you were yesterday, last month, last year or five minutes ago.

It is also important to understand that we may have certain traits or dispositions that make the incline of our manifesting journey much steeper – not impossible, just more challenging. You are unique. Your brain is unique. The wiring in your brain is unique. Neuroplasticity, discussed in depth in Chapter Three, refers to the brain's ability to change with learning. If I was asked to give an example of something plastic that I use regularly I would probably say my credit card or other items made from rigid plastic such as my toothbrush or my wheelie bin. To be honest, plastic of the flexible kind used to make plastic bags, toothpaste tubes or cling film wouldn't enter my head, so it took me a little while to get my head around the idea that to be plastic, in the context of the brain, means to be flexible, pliable, adaptable in the face of change. This ability to change is critical for manifesting. Neuroplasticity lies at the heart of what makes us human and what makes each of us different from everyone else. My brain and your brain may even differ in their capacity for neuroplasticity. As a consequence, the same experiences can produce different extents of neural learning and different types of plastic changes in your brain than in mine. Our brains are custom-built from the life experiences we have had since being in the womb. No one else's brain developed in exactly the same way as yours. Nor has anyone else had exactly the same experiences as you.

Your genetic profile is also unique and this together with developmental, experiential, social and economic differences impact all aspects of your psychology.

Let's take a closer look at how and why we differ; understanding this can help you to be compassionate towards yourself and stay motivated to attain change in the face of challenge. You and I are fundamentally the same in that we are both human. What does that mean? It means that we both have human DNA[ii] rather than dog DNA or cat DNA or ape DNA. The fact that I have human DNA means that I have a set of behavioural capacities and tendencies typical of humans that we generally refer to as 'human nature'. Some other species have similar capacities and tendencies to us, but these tend to be less developed in those species compared to humans. Many of our human capacities, such as the ability to walk upright, learn language and tell jokes, require development, learning and experience to mature, but the capacities themselves are inherent. We are born with the capacity to learn language, to learn how to walk, to develop a sense of humour.

Human nature, a product of evolution, provides us with species-specific tendencies and abilities, ensuring we act characteristically human, just as dogs act like dogs or cats like cats. This inherent nature is encoded in our DNA, not as a blueprint but more akin to a set of instructions. This set of genetic instructions shapes a human being's ability to interact with their environment. However, a genome is influenced by its environment, reflecting the life histories of its predecessors and the surroundings in which they existed. Hence we see an astounding diversity of humans, sharing common capacities but differing due to genetic variations, especially ones that occur during the reproduction process. These genetic differences can influence brain development and its functions, producing varying behavioural tendencies. Importantly, there aren't specific genes for particular traits like intelligence. The person we become is more than just the outcome of nature (genes) and nurture (environment); it's a complex interplay between factors involving the randomness of developmental processes, starting from the womb.

Brain development is an intricate journey, beginning at conception and continuing into young adulthood. While the early stages in the womb have a strong genetic underpinning, external factors like nutrition, maternal stress and other environmental elements can leave an imprint. Especially in infancy, the brain is incredibly plastic, undergoing rapid growth and fine-tuning, significantly influenced by positive or negative experiences. During puberty and extending into the mid-twenties, the brain undergoes transformative development, moulding cognitive abilities and behaviour. During this crucial phase, both nurturing and adverse environments play pivotal roles in shaping resilience, cognitive traits and emotional health. This means that our psychological composition is a product of an intricate interplay between genetics, environment and the unpredictability of developmental processes. Understanding how I became me and how you became you can inform our unique manifesting journeys.

Traits

When we think about how we became who we are we tend to attribute certain traits to our genetic heritage. We commonly talk about inheriting physical traits; you may have grown up being told that you got your mum's eyes, your dad's height and your grandmother's chin. We also talk about some psychological traits in a similar way – you may have been told you've got your dad's temper, your mum's smarts and your granny's creativity. There is a general acceptance that, in addition to inheriting physical features, at least some of our psychological traits are written in our DNA. The American Psychological Association's dictionary reflects this

dual application of the word 'trait' to both physical and psychological aspects of who we are by giving two definitions:[4]

1. an enduring personality characteristic that describes or
   determines an individual's behaviour across a range of
   situations.
2. in genetics, an attribute resulting from a hereditary predisposition (e.g. hair colour, facial features).

The NIH Human Genome Research Institute describes a 'trait'
as a distinct characteristic of an individual, which can be influenced
by genetics, the environment, or both. Traits can be things like eye
colour or more measurable qualities like height or stable, unique
brain features called neural traits.

So, where does our uniqueness stem from if our genome merely
encodes a 'human' rather than an individual? Consider height.
While our genome provides instructions for a typical human height,
individual genes can cause variations, making some of us taller or
shorter – but within human norms. Similarly, our behaviours and abilities, our psychological traits, are moulded by our genes. They provide
a template for human nature, but individual variations occur due to
unique genetic sequences in each of us. The specific genes we inherit
can influence how our brains develop and function, which in turn
affects our capabilities and our tendencies to behave in certain ways.

It is essential to note that our genetic differences don't mean
one person has a specific gene that another lacks. Extroversion,
for example, is highly heritable, but this doesn't mean that there
is a specific extrovert gene. If you're more extroverted than I am,
it's mainly due to genetic variations that influence your brain's

---

4 The APA dictionary actually offers a third definition related to 'item response theory', which is
beyond the scope of this book, and not relevant to the topic at hand.

development. Some of our psychological differences are 'pre-wired' during our brain's growth in the womb. But it's not just genes; our experiences and the process of development further shape us. Embracing these distinctions is crucial for personal growth and avoiding unhelpful comparisons.

Development

Identical twins[iii] develop from the same egg and the same DNA. However, despite starting out with identical DNA, by the time they are born they will not only have slightly different DNA, they will also each use their DNA differently. These changes can occur in parts of the DNA that affect how the identical twins look, resulting in, for example, slight differences in physical traits such as hair colour or the shape of their eyes, ears or nose. Some identical twins are mirror opposites of each other, with for example dimples or moles appearing on the right side in one twin and on the left in the other, or cowlicks might curl clockwise in one twin and counter-clockwise in the other. This means that, even when the initial genetic code is identical, the outcome won't be. It also illustrates the influence of development in the womb on DNA. Other DNA changes might happen in parts of the DNA that don't affect physical appearance. The physical structure of the brains of identical twins, especially at the cellular level, won't be identical. Developmental processes display significant levels of randomness at the molecular level and this means that the outcome can't be predicted precisely. The progressive nature of developmental processes means that the inherent variability in the physical structure of the brain together with genetic differences can have considerable effects on the outcome, contributing substantially to differences in who we are.

Heritability

Studies comparing identical with fraternal twins and biological with adoptive siblings help pinpoint the factors influencing variance in specific traits. If identical twins show closer similarities in a trait than fraternal twins, it's a clue to stronger genetic influence. However, when both adoptive and biological siblings share similarities in a trait, it suggests a predominant role of the family environment. Heritability studies delve into understanding these differences. However, a common misconception is that a high heritability percentage, for example, 80 per cent, means 80 per cent of that trait in a person is genetic. In truth, it means 80 per cent of variations from the average value of a trait in a given population is due to genetics. It's vital to understand that heritability is population-specific and changes based on varying external factors.

Heritability is often muddled with heredity, but they differ. While heredity refers to the gene transfer from parent to child, heritability is a statistical measure of genetic influences on a trait. Some traits arise from a unique combination of multiple genetic factors, and fresh mutations can also play a role. Numerous studies reveal that heritability for psychological traits ranges from 30 per cent to 80 per cent. This broad spectrum encompasses traits like intelligence, sleep patterns, marital fidelity and susceptibility to substance misuse, indicating the diverse ways our brains are wired. Although these traits remain stable, they can change – a fact often overlooked in discussions about personal growth and development. Let's take the example of Tina, an individual with a strong tendency towards anxiety. Tina wishes to manifest a future where she is no longer afraid of making presentations at work. Tina will have to work harder and longer than another individual who also wants to improve their presenting ability but who doesn't have a strong tendency towards anxiety.

Most of the manifesting material that I have read implies that manifesting is equally easy for all of us. The point I want to make here is that, while manifesting is feasible for all of us, our manifesting journeys will follow different trajectories due to differences in underlying psychological and other traits. Some journeys will be more challenging and take longer than others. Take, for instance, Sarah and her boyfriend, Alan, who both want to manifest better health. Their action plan includes regular exercise, a well-balanced diet and healthier sleep habits. Sarah, with a genetic predisposition towards insomnia, might find their plans more difficult to implement than Alan, who is not predisposed to insomnia. Sarah's insomnia makes it more likely that she will crave sugary, fatty foods, making it more difficult to stick to the healthy food plan. In addition, low energy levels caused by disrupted sleep make her less enthusiastic about exercise than Alan. This genetic inclination could make Sarah's journey to better health more complex and more challenging. Being aware of her genetic tendency and its knock-on effects could help Sarah desist from comparing her progress to Alan's and may spur her on to seek professional help to address her insomnia.

Many psychological traits have a genetic component, meaning that they're influenced by the genes we inherit from our parents. However, the environment also plays a crucial role in shaping these traits. For example, the big five personality traits – agreeableness, conscientiousness, extraversion, neuroticism and openness – have a heritability estimate of 40 to 60 per cent, which means that 40 to 60 per cent of the variation in these traits can be explained by genetic differences, with the remainder explained by environmental factors, developmental factors and individual experiences.

MRI scans and the measurements that can be extracted from them show that people who are genetically more similar to each other also have brains that are structurally more similar. At first glance, brain scans of identical twins look identical structurally, but a closer look reveals subtle differences. This is similar to the way that the faces of identical twins look identical at first glance but closer inspection can reveal subtle difference. Twin studies have given us fascinating insights into the brain. For instance, they've found that traits like total brain volume, grey matter (the brain cells) and white matter (the connections between these cells) are largely heritable. Delving deeper, there's also a noticeable heritability in the organisation of our individual neural pathways and how effectively the networks in our brains process information. So, nature plays a pretty significant role in shaping our brain's structure and function!

Taken together this shows that a lot, but not all, of the physical differences between how your brain and my brain are wired can be attributed to our genetic differences. Of course the genetic influence on wiring is not confined to the brain development that occurs within the womb. The genetic programme for brain development continues after birth and on to our early twenties, giving plenty of opportunity for further variation to arise.

The brain at rest

Understanding the anatomy of the brain and how it works when engaged in specific activities is absolutely fascinating and useful in terms of gaining self-awareness in the service of manifesting. But it is equally fascinating and useful to understand what the brain is doing when it is not focused on a specific task or activity. Your brain doesn't just come alive or fire up when you are actively doing something, it is constantly active, humming away in the background.

What is going on in your brain when you are not actively engaged in a task? Can the spontaneous neuronal activity that occurs when the brain is at rest tell us anything about who we are and our conscious experience of 'self'? Scientists have learned from research that there is inherent activity that occurs in an organised way in our brains when we are not actively engaged in a task. This organised neural activity allows the brain to be optimally ready to spring into action in response to internal and external stimuli.

I wish there was another word for stimuli. I know when I attended university I struggled at first to understand what the word really meant and whether it had any real-world validity, especially as I had only ever heard it used in the context of experiments. Stimulus is not really a word that we use every day, is it? It took me a while to get my head around the idea that it simply describes any change, experience or thing in the external or internal environment that evokes a functional reaction in a tissue, organ or organism (e.g. a human). For example, a noise (stimulus) will evoke a response in the parts of the brain that are responsible for processing auditory information (stimuli). A stimulus refers to something that arouses activity or energy. It acts like a spur to action or an incentive. Internal stimuli like hunger, thirst or feelings of loneliness let us know that we need to drink, eat or get socially connected and motivate us to take action to seek water, food or the company of others.

In order to be ready to respond to rapidly changing external or internal input or stimuli, brain networks need to reorganise into different patterns on a sub-second timescale. When your brain is at rest, when it's not focused on a specific task, different parts of it oscillate at different frequencies, producing brainwaves.

The adult EEG is often broken down into four frequency bands (see table below), which are associated with various states of consciousness (deep sleep, drowsiness, relaxed wakefulness and alert attention. A fifth band (gamma, >30Hz) has been associated with certain cognitive and motor functions. In a healthy, awake adult brain at rest with eyes closed the most prominent component of the EEG is the alpha rhythm. Considerable research has been carried out to identify the different features of these brainwaves and the functional roles they might play.

Frequency	Name	State
Delta	0–4Hz	Deep sleep
Theta	4–8Hz	Drowsiness
Alpha	8–12 or 13Hz	Relaxed wakefulness
Beta	12–30Hz	Alert attentiveness

Your brain is always active, whether you are responding to a stimulus or not, whether you are actively engaged in a task or not and whether you are asleep or awake. When you are awake and your brain is at rest, when it's not focused on a specific task, parts of your brain oscillate at different frequencies. The oscillations in each area become slightly stronger then weaker every ten to twenty seconds. When neuroscientists track these fluctuations across different areas of the brain while a person rests in a brain scanner for five minutes, they can identify which areas of the brain fluctuate in synchrony with each other. If two areas fluctuate in synchrony it's thought that they have a coactivation history and so are part of an extended functional network in the brain. While a general pattern of activity emerges, there are also individual differences.

Repeated imaging of the same people show that these differences are highly reliable and reflect stable differences in the functional architecture of the person's brain and the pattern of their brain activity. These neural traits are so distinctive that they have been referred to as 'neural fingerprints'. This research reveals that the brains of people who are genetically related are wired similarly and function similarly. From that it can be inferred that a considerable proportion of the variance in psychological and brain traits are due to genetic differences. It is important to note that, while neural traits are reliably stable, they are not immutable. They can be changed. For example meditation, repeated training on a task and neurofeedback can bring about changes to volume or baseline activation in targeted brain regions.

Consciousness

Manifesting raises awareness of the conscious self and encourages intentional action. The human brain, your brain, my brain, everyone's brains are electrical networks and chemical organs embedded in our bodies. Your experience of 'self', of being you, of being alive is created by a biological, electro-chemical process. Conscious experience is produced by the combined activity of the 86 billion neurons in your brain. Unless a person is under anaesthetic or living with a disease or disorder or specific type of brain injury that disturbs consciousness, they will have a sense of self, an enduring 'me-ness' that has existed for as long as they can remember. How can the rich inner, subjective experience of self be explained by the nuts and bolts, or rather the blood and guts, or more precisely the cells and chemical messengers in the brain and the body? How do the many facets of consciousness relate to and depend on neuronal processes carried out by those cells and through those connections and their interactions with our internal and external worlds?

Conscious experience seems to us to be continuous. However, research actually shows that conscious mental activity is not continuous and can be broken down into a series of states that present as discrete patterns of neuronal activity across the whole brain. These states, referred to as microstates, last for only fractions of a second. Scientists suggest that these microstates represent the basic building blocks of consciousness. Some scientists even refer to microstates as the 'atoms of thought'. Scientists propose that resting-state microstates measure individual differences in how our core neural networks work.

When our state of consciousness is altered due to sleep, anaesthetic, meditation or psychiatric diseases the dynamics of microstates also change. Consciousness can shift due to sleep, meditation or other states. Understanding how these shifts influence the manifestation process might offer further insights into both how manifesting works and the nature of consciousness. Meditation and mindfulness, techniques associated with manifesting, are often used as a way to quiet our inner voice and focus on our intentions. Since the dynamics of microstates can change with meditation, understanding these shifts could potentially, in time, with more research, offer insight into the neurological basis of these and other manifesting practices.

Without conscious experience, there is nothing. There is no you. There is no reality. There is no 'self' to help, no 'self' to improve. There is no 'you' to manifest a better version. There is no 'you' to live that best life. There is no reality to change. There is no external world to inhabit and no internal world to experience. Without consciousness, or more specifically without consciousness of 'self', would manifesting matter? I think not. There would be no 'self' to have desires or dreams to manifest, there would be no 'self' to wish, to plan, to act, to experience.

What can neuroscience tell us about conscious experience? Before the development of contemporary brain-imaging technology, the only option available to neuroscientists trying to understand how the brain works was to study the structural and functional changes that occur as a consequence of damage to specific brain structures, caused by injury, stroke, infection or neurological disease.

John Hughlings Jackson, a researcher working at the end of the nineteenth century, noted that epileptic seizures that arose in specific areas of the brain were sometimes accompanied by changes in conscious experience. He proposed that consciousness was the highest level of brain organisation and involved interactions between conscious and unconscious processes. This early re-search still influences neuroscientific and psychological study of consciousness.

Consciousness is about experience. The administration of a profound, general anaesthetic almost completely shuts down the electrical activity in the brain and consciousness becomes completely absent. You have no experience of the time spent under anaesthetic. You have no subjective experience of self. You, your conscious self, ceases to exist. Going under general anaesthetic is probably the closest a human can get to 'experiencing' death while still being alive. I've put 'experiencing' in inverted commas because being under general anaesthetic makes it impossible to experience anything because the state it produces is the complete absence of conscious experience, the complete absence of conscious self. It is nothingness.

The idea of death as 'nothingness' is quite a comforting thought for me. That, of course, is not the same as saying I want to die. Nothing could be further from the truth. I'm in love with life and most certainly not ready for the experience to end, but I can take comfort in the fact that when my life does end I will no longer experience anything at all, pleasant or unpleasant. Once death takes me, there will be no pain because there will be no 'me' to experience pain.

Pain is a conscious experience. You must be conscious to experience it. Pain is not something external to you. It is not a property of the external world in the same way that heat and cold and wetness are. Of course, there will be no joy, or happiness, or love either but since consciousness will be entirely absent I will not experience their loss. For a child raised to fear the eternal fires of hell and the suffering of purgatory, nothingness seems like a very pleasant option.

I was also raised to believe in the carrot of heaven, an afterlife that would be my reward for never having sinned. Like others, I've wondered about stories of near-death experiences, but I am very comfortable with the knowledge that the oft-referred-to light at the end of a tunnel is not a portal to the afterlife but rather the result of the brain's visual system being deprived of oxygen. I am acutely aware that the notion of an afterlife gives people great comfort and my intention is not to take that away. Everyone is entitled to believe whatever they wish, especially if it helps them through grief and loss, as long as it causes no harm.

The study of consciousness goes back thousands of years and was initially the preserve of philosophers who debated its nature. It is only in recent years that technology has allowed neuroscientists' to explore this phenomenon at the level of brain cells. In 1994, physicist and molecular biologist Francis Crick, the co-discoverer of molecular DNA, wrote the following: 'You, your joys and your sorrows, your memories and your ambitions, your sense of personal identity and free will, are in fact no more than the behaviour of a vast assembly of nerve cells and their associated molecules.' Personally,

I find this incredibly exciting. The 'no more than' in the sentence is a little misleading as 'no more than' sort of implies that it is no big deal. But the point that I believe Crick was trying to make is that there is no need to look outside ourselves for some external, mystical force responsible for the conscious experience of being alive when everything that creates the magical experience of being human lies within us, within our brains. How amazing is that?

Neuroscience and psychology, like other sciences, have their roots in philosophy and as a consequence it is difficult to talk about the neuroscience of the conscious experience of self without taking account of philosophical positions about the human condition that have had enduring influence on science, language, culture, religion and our world views. Of particular interest is dualism, where a definitive categorical distinction is drawn between mental and physical; mind and matter; body and soul; spiritual and corporeal; the material and the immaterial.

Dualism is at odds with the default assumption of many neuroscientists that all that exists is ultimately physical. In this view, the universe is made of physical stuff. Conscious states, including our conscious experience of 'self', emerge from or are identical to specific arrangements of physical stuff in our brains and our bodies. The philosopher Descartes separated mind and matter, drawing a distinction between mind (consciousness) and matter (physical stuff), arguing that they are different substances. The interesting thing about Cartesian dualism is its seductive nature. Doesn't it seem to make intuitive sense? After all, our sense of self, our conscious experience of self, feels non-physical. This type of dualism to this day drives our beliefs, usually unconsciously. Descartes' philosophy was transformational for science, and, despite the fact that few philosophers or scientists today would explicitly align themselves with Cartesian dualism, its influence can still be felt in our daily lives through science, medicine and wider Western culture. One example of particular note is the separation of neurological (physical matter) conditions and psychiatric (mind) disorders in medicine.

The idea – the feeling – that we have a thinking soul at our core that gives rise to our conscious experience of an unchanging, immaterial self that originated in ancient philosophy persists today. While philosophy can seem very academic, it does throw some light on why we think the way we do about our conscious experience of self and the universe. It illuminates our tendency towards this brand of dualism that separates mind and body. It explains why it can feel somewhat challenging to accept the monistic view of neuroscience that our conscious experience of self comes from the physical substance of our brains and our bodies.

Brain imaging technology has allowed neuroscientists to understand that the brain is not one single, indivisible organ, but rather is a collection of billions of individual cells communicating via a complex system of trillions of connections organised into specialising networks and functional divisions. This technology allows neuroscientists to explore the brain as the source of self-awareness, which is critical to manifesting. Using fMRI scanning, neuroscientists have been able to identify the brain networks that become active when we reflect on the self. Stephen M. Fleming, author of *Know Thyself: The New Science of Self-Awareness*, describes our capacity for self-awareness as the brain pulling off 'this marvellous conjuring trick'. The study of self-awareness is a perfect example of how magic explained becomes science.

Scientific study of consciousness and the brain began in the late nineteenth century with psychological research questions emerging from philosophical understanding of 'the mind', a concept often considered synonymous with consciousness. The American

Psychological Association broadly defines 'the mind' as all intellectual and psychological happenings, the totality of your mental and psychological processes and the structural and functional cognitive components on which they depend, including cognitive, behavioural, motivational, emotional and perceptual systems. More narrowly, the mind can be viewed as referring to just cognitive activities and functions (e.g. thinking, remembering, attending, language, learning, problem-solving, etc.). The nature of the relationship between 'the mind' and the body, of which the brain is, of course, a part, remains the subject of ongoing debate, thanks mainly to Descartes and his Cartesian dualism, which separated mind and matter. Countless experts from multiple disciplines have wrestled with the 'mind–body' problem his dualism created, i.e. how to account for the relationship between mental and physical processes. Solutions to the problem include; interactionalism[iv], parallelism[v], idealism[vi], double-aspect theory[vii], epiphenomenalism[viii], and materialism[ix].

The concept of 'the mind' is a hangover from philosophical musings from a past long before neuroscience increased our understanding of the human brain and its role in all that we do, feel and think. The mind is really just a linguistic construct to explain our conscious experience of self. For me, it is an unnecessary middleman that serves only to confuse, particularly when 'the mind', which is an abstract concept, is seen as something concrete; a thing rather than a process. My view is that the abstract concept of 'the mind' describes our conscious experience. When we remove the concept of 'the mind' we can focus directly on how the human body, including the brain, brings about our conscious experience of a person who can think, feel, love, learn and laugh. I don't have all of the answers, but I think this simplifies things. Neuroscience offers real insight into mental and psychological processes including consciousness and our experience of self.

Self-Perception

We tend to believe that what we perceive is how things are in real time. But we know from neuroscience that this is not the case. The 86 billion cells and trillions of connections in your brain work together to generate your conscious experience of the world around you. Your perceptions of the world are essentially your brain's best guess, based on a combination of your brain's predictions informed by information accumulated over time together with your brain's interpretation of the multitude of incoming, often ambiguous, electrical signals from the outside world and from inside your body. This means that you don't passively consume what is in the world, you actively create your conscious experience of the world. Your brain generates your reality. This is the neuroscience of how you manifest your reality. You are living a story that has been created by your brain. Most of the time the story matches reality, but not always.

Adaptability is the key to survival and critical for managing change, which, at the end of the day, is what manifesting is about. One of the most important adaptations is the brain's ability to simulate and predict potential outcomes and rapidly respond in the face of change, challenge, threat or opportunity. The brain uses past experiences to predict outcomes, and when these expectations don't match the incoming signal, a prediction error occurs, triggering learning and adaptability. The more the brain can minimise the difference between its predicted outcome and the incoming signal, the better the brain will be at anticipating and responding efficiently and effectively.

Think of the brain as a city government that uses historical records to forecast what might happen next. When the city's predictions don't match the reports coming in from the outside (like weather forecasts versus actual weather), that's like a prediction error. This discrepancy causes the city government (the brain) to learn and adapt, adjusting its strategies and policies. The closer the city's forecasts are to the actual reports coming in, the better the city will be at preparing and responding. It's the same with the brain. The better your brain gets at making accurate predictions, the better it will be at anticipating and responding effectively to the world around you, which, in turn, increases the likelihood of successful manifesting.

Let's look at what happens when we perceive a moving object, such as a ball moving through space. Once the light from the ball hits your retina the incoming signals are converted into electrical signals that are transmitted to the visual cortex at the back of your brain and onwards to the front of your brain where perceptions are formed. This process takes hundreds of milliseconds, during which time the ball has moved on to another location. This time lag means that the incoming information about the location of the ball is already outdated by the time you consciously perceive it.

Let's say the moving object is a baseball being thrown back and forth between two people, à la the famous episode of *Friends*, 'The One With the Ball', where Ross and Joey play 'catch' for two hours to avoid boredom. For Joey (or Ross) to successfully catch the moving ball, their brains must compensate for the processing time by anticipating the current position of the ball along a predictable trajectory. The brain accounts for the time lag caused by neural processing, by extrapolating the trajectory of the ball into the future.

To avoid being hit by the ball and to increase our chances of catching the ball the brain predicts the likely path of motion before it happens. To allow for the time lag, the brain makes a best guess about where the ball ought to be now, rather than where it was when the visual information first hit your retina. We perceive moving things ahead of their path of motion. This ability to predict makes humans more coordinated and more accurate, allowing Joey and Ross to play catch for two hours without dropping the ball. What we consciously experience as reality is not a real-time reflection of reality. Prediction is adaptive, allowing us to avoid injury and life-threatening scenarios, such as being run over by a car while crossing the road. It also allows us to anticipate risk and opportunity on our manifesting journey.

Most of our conscious experience involves brain predictions and guesswork, as our brain interprets and creates our experience of reality. This is where the facets of manifesting that work on changing expectations and clearly articulating desires play a role in how we perceive and shape our reality.

The predictions and estimates your brain produces are only as good as the data on which they are based. If the data is outdated, inaccurate, biased, compromised or irrelevant then your brain's predictions – for example, about what you can achieve on your manifesting journey or your capacity to cope in the face of challenges – will be meaningless and inaccurate. The practice of manifesting helps people to examine this data and replace it with information that is less self-limiting and more empowering. This then influences the brain's predictions, for example upgrading your estimations of what you can achieve and what is possible to manifest.

Our perceptions of the world, life, events, experiences, people and indeed of our selves are not simply a reflection of an external reality. Perception is neither passive nor objective. Perceiving the world is an active brain process influenced by multiple factors. The brain's use of guesswork and predictions, informed by sensory signals, to create our reality is functional and useful. From a manifesting perspective it is important to remember that the brain's predictions are not necessarily accurate, especially if you tend towards limiting beliefs or negative perceptions.

The self is a pretty special type of perception; despite this it is still just a best guess, but one that evolved to keep you alive. When it comes to thinking of self, most of us have biases. It seems natural to think of 'self' as something that exists, an actual thing rather than a collection of perceptions. However, when we intuit an actual self we are leaning towards Cartesian dualism wherein this actual self is indivisible and unchangeable. It is challenging to think otherwise; it feels right, the idea of an actual self really resonates psychologically, especially for those of us raised in Western societies.

The concept of the 'self' is fascinating, capable of unravelling or distorting under the influence of various diseases and disorders. Dementia, delirium, schizophrenia, amnesia, phantom limb syndrome, out-of-body experiences and other peculiarly named conditions allow us to see through the window of symptoms into the multifaceted nature of our sense of self.

Scientific examination of these intriguing phenomena reveals that our experience of self is not a singular entity, but rather a delicate fusion of several interwoven elements. It is a finely crafted masterpiece, where the various components seamlessly blend together to form our unique sense of conscious experience. The journey of self-discovery is a fascinating one. We often perceive our sense of self as this singular, continuous entity, as if there's an unchanging self hidden behind our eyes, steering our bodies and actions. However, the truth is far more intriguing. Our sense of self is a complex interplay of multiple elements, despite the illusion of a unified whole.

In his thought-provoking book *Being You*, Anil Seth delves into the intricate nature of the human self, shedding light on its various facets from the experience of being or having a body to personal identity (e.g. mother, daughter, artist, scientist). Seth breaks down the components of the human self into distinct elements, each contributing to our overall experience: the embodied self, the perspectival self, the volitional self, the narrative self and the social self. These elements, like puzzle pieces, come together to shape our understanding of who we are.

The embodied self describes the profound sensation of being alive and connected to your physical body, including feeling emotions and moods. It is actually more than a feeling, it is a conviction that you identify with and own your body. This is not something we experience with other objects in the world, even those of which we have ownership. The precarious nature of the embodied self is evident in phantom limb syndrome where, following amputation of a limb, the individual can feel their amputated limb as if it were still there.

The perspectival self is a bit of a mouthful, but it just refers to the feeling that we have a unique perspective and viewpoint on the world that sits just behind our eyes, allowing us to view the world and some of our body from that specific position. When you close one eye that view will include the side of your nose; with both eyes open your nose is less obvious. I stupidly got sunburned at the weekend and my nose is now peeling, and as a consequence a little piece of peeling skin is annoyingly popping into the forefront of my first-person perspective.

Out-of-body experiences (OBEs), sensations of floating outside one's body, were once deemed mystical, but modern neuroscience offers biological explanations. One theory highlights the role of the temporal-parietal junction (TPJ), an area in the brain vital for integrating sensory information. Disruptions to the TPJ, whether from injury, epilepsy or other causes, can lead to a disconnection between body perception and world perception, often resulting in OBEs. Additionally, experiments with virtual reality have demonstrated that tricking the brain about body location can create OBE-like experiences. OBEs have been linked to various conditions, including migraines, sleep deprivation, drug use and near-death experiences. Despite these insights, the exact cause of OBEs remains elusive and, while people have reported such experiences for millennia, current evidence supports the notion that OBEs are likely a glitch in brain functioning, not an escape of an immaterial self or soul. Future research may uncover the specific mechanisms involved.

The volitional self comes into play when we make choices and exert what is commonly referred to as our willpower. It refers to the feeling of causing things to happen or intending to do things. This volitional self plays a big role in manifesting; setting intentions and then taking action to make these intentions a reality.

The narrative self weaves together our autobiographical memories, our memories of past events and the stories we tell ourselves about our past, present and future. The hippocampi are relatively small structures (I've used the plural because you have two, one in each hemisphere) in the limbic brain (see fig. 7) that play a big role in memory, allowing us to lay down new memories and access old ones. We know from patients who have sustained substantial injury to the hippocampi in both the right and left hemispheres that without them we would no longer be able to string together a narrative sense of self over time because we would no longer have access to memories of events in our life, including those involving ourselves. As a consequence we would have no continuous sense of self. Every few seconds or so, it would be as if our life were to begin again from scratch with no recollection of our former life or self. To paraphrase Oscar Wilde, memory is the diary that we all carry about with us.

Let's now look at the social self, which is about how I perceive others perceiving me. It emerges in childhood and continues to evolve across our lives. It also brings with it a range of new emotional possibilities tied to social interaction such as guilt, shame, pride, love and belonging.

Our ability to perceive the intentions, beliefs and desires of others is always operating in the background in our brains. This ability shapes our thinking, behaviour and feelings and guides our social interactions. The experience of being you depends a great deal on how you perceive others perceiving you. A lot of this occurs without conscious awareness, just as effortlessly as when we perceive dogs, cats, motorbikes and muffins.

Perceiving ourselves through the lens of other's viewpoints is foundational to our social identity in ways that can help or hinder us on our manifesting journey. When it comes to manifesting, our social interactions and the way we perceive others' thoughts and intentions are intricately intertwined. By understanding how others might interpret our desires, goals and actions, we can gain valuable insights. Our social identity and the dynamics of our relationships shape our manifesting journey. The way we interact with others, the support and encouragement we receive and the feedback we incorporate all contribute to our growth and development. By recognising the impact of our social environment on our manifestation process, we can cultivate positive relationships and surround ourselves with individuals who uplift and inspire us, further propelling us towards manifesting the best version of ourselves.

Imagine you are walking down a street in your neighbourhood when you spot a local resident you've never met but have seen in the vicinity on a number of occasions. As this person approaches, you notice their friendly smile. As they begin to raise their hand, you intuitively understand that they're about to greet you with a wave. Without any words being exchanged, you effortlessly perceive their intention to acknowledge your presence.

Social perception is a bit trickier than non-social perception; we'll rarely confuse a motorbike with a milk bottle, but we can get things very wrong when perceiving what's going on inside someone else's head. There are multiple opportunities to get it wrong because the sensory signals from which we infer someone else's mental state or emotions have to pass through various stages, such as facial expressions, gestures, body language and aspects of speech.

Social perceptions are context and expectation dependent. Social prediction errors can be minimised by updating predictions or via a process known as active inference (discussed in detail in the next chapter) to alter the sensory signals so that they match the prediction or our desires. I am an avid fan of smiling and try to insert my smiling advice into my books and talks; here I will use it to illustrate active inference in a social situation. Smiling is somewhat contagious; it's difficult not to respond to a smile with a smile. If I expect someone to be pleased to see me and I arrive to find they have a cross or gloomy face rather than a welcoming one I can crack a smile and be confident in the knowledge that they will automatically smile back. In this case I have not only changed the social situation to match my prediction I have actually impacted on the other person's mood, since smiling releases feel-good hormones.

Our ability to infer other people's mental states requires the generation of guesses about sensory signals. In the case of social perception this means making educated guesses about what others might be thinking, feeling or planning. This process is highly interactive. For example, the best way for me to understand what you are thinking is to consider how you might understand what I am thinking. This means I can only grasp your thoughts if I try to understand how you are interpreting my thoughts. This is how we see ourselves from other viewpoints. This is the essence of our social identity and these socially nestled predictive perceptions play a big role in your human experience and in your manifesting journey towards the best version of yourself.

In addition to the positive impact of social perceptions on our manifesting journey, it's important to acknowledge that there can also be negative influences at play. Negative social perceptions, such as judgements, criticism or limiting beliefs projected onto us by others, can hinder our manifestation process. If we internalise these negative perceptions, they can shape our own thoughts and beliefs, leading to self-doubt, resistance or a lack of confidence in our abilities to manifest our desires. These negative influences can create barriers and prevent us from fully embracing our potential and manifesting our goals.

Furthermore, social dynamics can sometimes lead us to make comparisons that lead to feelings of inadequacy. Seeing others' achievements or progress may trigger feelings of envy or a sense of falling behind, which can negatively impact our manifesting journey. These emotions can generate doubt, insecurity and a lack of focus on our own unique path, diverting our energy away from creating our desired reality.

Unsupportive or toxic relationships can impede our manifestation efforts. Negative influences from individuals who undermine our dreams, dismiss our abilities or discourage our aspirations can dampen our belief in ourselves and hinder our progress. It is essential to recognise these detrimental influences and prioritise surrounding ourselves with supportive, uplifting and encouraging individuals who genuinely believe in our potential to manifest and thrive.

By acknowledging the potential negative impact of social perceptions and dynamics, we can consciously choose to minimise their influence on our manifestation journey. Cultivating self-awareness, practising self-compassion, setting healthy boundaries and consciously selecting positive social connections can help mitigate these negative effects and facilitate clarity, allowing us to stay focused, empowered and aligned with our manifesting goals.

Ultimately, understanding both the positive and negative aspects of social perceptions within our manifesting journey enables us to navigate these influences consciously, harness the positive and minimise the negative, empowering us to manifest our desires and become the best version of ourselves.

It's remarkable to consider how these distinct elements knit together, creating the rich tapestry of our sense of self. The next time you reflect on who you are, remember that beneath the illusion of a singular, unchanging self lies a beautifully complex amalgamation of these diverse elements that are a collection of perceptions seamlessly woven together from a neural skein of predictions geared towards keeping you alive. It's an awe-inspiring feat, really, and one that we often take for granted in the hustle and bustle of everyday life. Pause and contemplate the sheer complexity of your own consciousness . . . It's pretty amazing.

Now that the foundations are laid, it's time to take concrete action for change.

PART TWO

CONSTRUCTION

Change

*'The secret of change is to focus all of your energy not
on fighting the old but on building the new'*
Socrates

Brain Change

Manifesting is fundamentally about change. It's about changing
your thinking, your behaviour, your reality and your brain. In his
book *Manifesting Change*, best-selling author Mike Dooley shares
an anecdote from his book tour during which he took part in
more than seventy radio interviews (I know that feeling). He was
repeatedly asked what keeps people from living their dream life.
Mike's response was always the same: not understanding the
nature of reality, who you are or how to make change happen.
Following on from our in-depth look at who we are in Chapter
Two, this chapter explores what neuroscience can tell us about
the mechanisms of change and the nature of reality.

Your brain can change itself. Our brains come pre-wired but
they are not hard-wired. Your brain circuitry at the molecular
level is highly plastic; that means it is flexible and can change in

response to the world around you and the world within you. Your brain is constantly changing, shaped by the things that you do, think, feel and experience. This innate neuroplasticity underlies human adaptability and resilience. That is how our brains record our experiences, our memories and the causes, effects and patterns we observe in the world for future reference, all the while making value judgements about outcomes and whether to repeat or avoid them. Anything you have ever learned through experience brought about a change in the connections between certain neurons in your brain. That change in neural connections will alter your response to the situation when you encounter it again. Learning from experience, aka neuroplasticity, physically changes our brains, affects our behaviour and shapes our reality.

Neuroplasticity bestows on us the ability to actively shape our reality by rewiring our brain circuitry. Manifesting practices tap into this ability to help us adapt and change in the service of our goals. We are how we predictably think, feel and behave. Many of these patterns of behaving, thinking and feeling were wired in childhood. They have been repeatedly and automatically firing together for so long that they feel as if they are an unchangeable part of who we are. But they are not inherent. They are learned. It is the capacity for change, for neuroplasticity, that is inherent, not the specific learned patterns of thinking, feeling or behaving. Manifesting steps such as aligning your thinking and behaviour with your vision, together with techniques that support learning, harness neuroplasticity and replace old patterns with new focused ones, are what will propel you towards your manifesting goals.

When you try something new, learn a new skill or a new way of behaving, new connections are built in your brain. The more you practise or repeat this new skill or new way of behaving, the stronger these connections become. Research indicates that some manifesting techniques (e.g. affirmations, positive thinking and 'acting as if') harness neuroplasticity to bring about change. This is not surprising really since neuroplasticity is the mechanism through which we adapt and acquire new knowledge and skills. Neuroplasticity is magnificent, but it doesn't have the magical powers I've seen ascribed to it in some content I've encountered online. Neuroplasticity is an amazing human capacity that has evolved to allow us to survive in, and adapt to, an ever-changing world. However, it cannot perform miracles or instantly transform your life, nor does it offer infinite possibility for change. Having said that, it is possible for neural pathways to be strengthened and new ones to be created, but this can require extensive training. The effective elements of manifesting that I identify in this book tap into neuroplasticity by acting like a training programme for changing your brain. Manifesting harnesses our innate neuroplasticity, allowing us to mould our experiences, memories and observations into a new framework for understanding and manifesting our desires. By leveraging the power of neuroplasticity, manifesting helps us to actively reshape our neural connections, modifying our responses, behaviours and, ultimately, our reality.

To effectively manifest, you need to embrace the possibility of **Change** then use the power of neuroplasticity to make it happen. Building a **Connection** with yourself to understand your learned patterns of thinking, feeling and behaving helps you to use manifesting techniques known to promote neuroplasticity in a targeted way. These manifesting techniques help you to learn new behaviours and lay down new neural pathways, switching limiting behaviours for focused ones that will take you closer to your goals. Having **Compassion** for yourself is critical because harnessing neuroplasticity as an adult requires considerable effort and specific circumstances, but it can be done. Changing ingrained habits, long-established patterns of responding, requires repetition, effort and patience because we know from neuroscience that big changes can take months, or longer.

Clarity is about having a clear vision for your future self. Visualisation, a technique commonly used to gain clarity about that which you wish to manifest, triggers many of the same neural regions as an actual experience, influencing you both physically and emotionally. Neurons activate and brain chemicals are released, whether an experience is real or imagined. From a brain perspective there is little difference between visualising an action and actually doing it. Visualisation can literally change your brain. Research has demonstrated that visualisation can alter neural pathways. **Coherence**, aligning your thoughts, feelings and actions with your vision, is not only critical for successfully manifesting change, but is also important for neuroplasticity. If you want to be healthier, for example, aligning thoughts (like self-belief), feelings (like motivation) and actions (like exercising) in sync will make it easier for learning and the associated brain changes to occur as each reinforces the other. Finally, to **Create** your new reality manifesting promotes the active use of tools like affirmations, visualisation and journaling, known to promote neuroplasticity, reinforcing new neural pathways, making them stronger, fostering positive change.

It is important to note that although neuroplasticity is usually adaptive, it can also be maladaptive; throughout our lives we can learn ways to behave in the world that have negative consequences, are unhealthy, unhelpful or self-limiting. Addiction can be thought of as a maladaptive form of learning, that changes the brain's reward and motivation circuits. Chronic pain can also be the result of maladaptive changes to the pain pathway. From puberty to about the age of twenty-five our brains go through a critical period of development where neuroplasticity is heightened. This enhanced ability to learn from experience is vital for becoming a mature, well-adapted adult. Unfortunately, the flip side of this extra-plastic period is that it makes us more vulnerable to addiction and mental illness through our teen and early adult years.

As you work through this book you may discover that some of the behaviours and thought patterns that you want to change are maladaptive. Let's take coping strategies as an example – adaptive strategies help to build resilience and make things better in both the short and long term. In contrast, maladaptive strategies may feel useful in the short term but only make matters worse in the longer term. Actively seeking solutions or support, altering your expectations, taking action/s to manage stress or changing how you view the stressor are all adaptive coping mechanisms. In contrast, maladaptive coping mechanisms can include some or several of the following: misuse of alcohol and other drugs, binge eating, rumination, excessive daydreaming, procrastination, avoidance, self-harm, self-blame, self-criticism and taking risks like engaging in unsafe sex. Be aware that change in these cases will be challenging and take more effort; successful change of maladaptive behaviours or thought patterns may require additional support from trained professionals and may benefit from treatment such as cognitive behavioural therapy.

Manifesting is about choosing a positive vision of your future and taking concrete action to transform that vision into a reality. As I explained in the introduction, manifesting is not a passive process nor is it wishful thinking: it requires conscious effort, choice, action, control, learning and behaviour change. What most people refer to as manifesting might better be described as 'conscious manifesting' to distinguish it from the kind of 'non-conscious manifesting' that most of us have been effortlessly engaging in all of our lives. Our brains continuously shape our reality and our future through prediction and under the ongoing influence of unconscious biases, habits and patterns of thinking and action, without conscious direction or oversight. In contrast, conscious manifesting is a process whereby a person consciously envisions a specific reality and transforms that vision into a tangible result through considered action and goal-directed behaviour.

Reality is an illusion performed by the brain. Your conscious experience is constructed by your brain. And your brain uses habits, shortcuts, guesswork and its powers of prediction to influence how you act. The considered and intentional action advocated in manifesting improves your brain's prediction powers and encourages the formation of more goal-directed habitual behaviours.

Action

Manifesting requires action. Ryuu Shinohara says that taking action is the most critical step for achieving your chosen manifesting goal. Action requires energy. Every action that we take relies on both physical and neural energy. The brain is the most energy-demanding organ. Like all other cells in the body, brain cells rely on glucose, a form of sugar, for energy. Complex carbohydrates from the food we eat are broken down into simple sugars by a small structure within each brain cell. Unlike muscles, the brain doesn't have a reserve supply of energy that it can draw on when demand increases. The brain has no way to store energy. This means that the brain needs a constant supply of oxygen and energy to keep its billions of brain cells alive. About a quarter of the brain's energy is used for general housekeeping and cell maintenance. The remaining energy is used for neural communication.

The primary function of neurons is to process and transmit

information along miles of neural cables and across trillions of synapses, which are the tiny gaps between brain cells where signals are sent and received.

Manifestation is all about taking effective action and changing your perceptions. Acting in the world and perceiving the world are inextricably linked. In fact, action and perception determine and define each other. We perceive the world to act effectively within it. Perception is critical for action. Every perception that we experience is the way it is to help guide our actions. In turn, every action alters our perception by changing incoming sensory signals. Understanding how the brain perceives reality and how you perceive the world is key to acting more effectively within it in pursuit of manifesting goals. Never forget though that the brain's primary function is to keep you alive. We perceive the world around us so that we can act in ways that increase our prospects of survival.

The human brain is hungry for knowledge, ceaselessly probing the environment that envelops it on a never-ending quest for understanding. Your brain not only generates your actions, it continually calibrates them using sensory input so that you can best achieve your goals. Manifesting works because steps such as clearly articulating and envisioning your goals help your brain make more accurate calibrations.

Reality

In his book *The Magic of Manifesting*, Ryuu Shinohara underscores the importance of comprehending the true nature of reality. He argues that understanding reality is fundamental to manifesting and questions how progress towards any goal could be made in the absence of this knowledge. What is reality? Despite the fact that we live it every day, when you think about it, really think about it, reality is hard to put into words. Neuroscientist Anil Seth adopts a utilitarian approach, arguing that we don't perceive reality as it actually is, instead we see it from a functional perspective – how we can use this incoming information from the world to our benefit. Philosophers have struggled to understand the concept for centuries, posing questions such as *if a tree falls in a forest with nobody there does it still make a noise?* Manifesting content that proffers quantum physics as the scientific basis for manifesting is pre-empting the outcome of science that hasn't happened yet, could possibly happen or may never happen. Quantum physics is still largely theoretical and the idea of using it to manifest specific outcomes is not widely accepted by the scientific community. This is one of the reasons that the practice of manifesting has been banished to the world of woo and away from the sphere of evidence-based science. Using quantum physics to justify or explain manifesting tends to oversimplify and misrepresent both the scientific concepts involved in quantum mechanics and the proactive, disciplined nature of manifesting.

Quantum mechanics, the study of the behaviour of the tiniest particles in our universe, has shown some strange phenomena like superposition, where particles can exist in multiple states simultaneously. These ideas have led to fascinating concepts. However, they are not well understood, especially with regard to how these concepts apply to larger objects in the classical world that we inhabit. Current experiments are a cycle of design and debate, and the scientific community is far from conclusive answers. I will leave further discussion and debate on this relationship to quantum physicists and those who extrapolate the science beyond existing scientific evidence. I will focus instead on what neuroscience can tell us about reality and about manifesting.

In her book, *Manifest*, Roxie Nafousi says, 'The science of manifesting works in another way, too, that is less about quantum physics and more about neuroscience.' As it happens, findings from neuroscience disrupt the commonly held view that there is an independent reality filled with things, people and places that all have properties (e.g. shape, size and colour). We tend to think that our senses convey this information about the objects we encounter in the world to the brain, whereupon the information is processed to become an accurate reflection – the reality that we perceive.

We have become accustomed to the idea that the brain is a sort of computer inside our skull that builds a picture of the outside world for the 'I' behind the eyes. This is what is known as a 'bottom-up' view of perception, where stimuli, such as light waves, sound waves and molecules conveying taste and smell, encountered by our sense organs, travel upwards or inwards to the brain via electrical signals. This bottom-up view of perception fits well with what we know about brain anatomy. For example, specific sense modalities such as sight and hearing are, broadly speaking, associated with specific anatomical regions of the brain, i.e. the visual cortex in the occipital lobe, and the auditory cortex in the temporal lobe (fig. 4).

Imagine your brain as a busy city. There are lots of different parts, or neighbourhoods, that each have their own function. One neighbourhood is where you process sound, another might be where you make decisions and so on. Now, when you're doing a specific task, like reading a book, the relevant neighbourhoods of your brain city 'light up' – they get busier because they're being used. While you read the book the parts of your brain involved in language comprehension, focus and perhaps imagination are all activated.

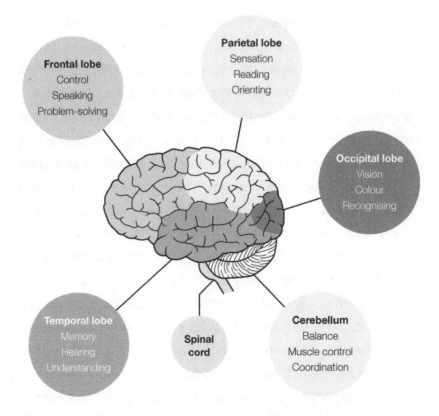

Fig. 4: Brain regions and overview of functions

Taking vision as an example, let's imagine our brain city again. This time, let's consider the brain areas involved in processing visual signals like a series of different departments in a city's government building, each responsible for processing different aspects of a visual scene. For our example, let's say you're looking at a park scene that has both a car and a cat. Closest to the city entrance (which represents our eyes or sensory input) are the early processing departments. These departments are like the basic processing offices, where they handle very fundamental, raw data such as differences in the level of illumination supplying information about edges and ultimately shapes like the outlines of the car or the cat. As we move further into the government building, we arrive at more specialised departments. Here, there are experts (brain cells) who focus on specific details from the early processing departments. These experts specialise in colour and fine detail, for example a car's wing mirror or a cat's whiskers. They process more specific aspects of the visual scene. Other experts focus on the movement of the cat or car. Even further into the building, we have the high-level departments. These are like the city planning offices. Here, experts interpret the specific details from earlier departments and put them together to form whole images and concepts. They can recognise objects and classify what they've received into categories like 'automobile' or 'animal' or even more specific ones like 'car' or 'cat' or 'Mercedes' or 'tabby cat' or 'my car' or 'Jason's cat'.

The key is that each department takes the visual signals processed by the department before it, pools that information together and then sends it on so that brain cells (experts) in higher levels can respond accordingly. In this way, the brain (or our city government building) can efficiently process visual signals in a hierarchical manner, moving from basic to more complex levels of understanding. Scientific experiments in animals and humans also support the bottom-up approach, with brain cells involved in the early stages of processing firing in response to simple features like edges, while brain cells at later stages respond to complex features like faces.

However, how things seem isn't always how they actually are. It seems that the sun turns round the earth, but we know from science that the earth revolves in orbit around the sun. Knowing this doesn't change how the sun seems – it still looks like the sun goes around the earth.

While it can appear that our perception of the world is driven by incoming data (bottom up), in all likelihood it is actually derived from higher-order cognitive processes like memory, knowledge and expectations (top down). Top-down processing means the brain takes the incoming data, applies what it knows and what it expects to perceive and fills in the gaps. Knowing this won't change how the world seems but it will dramatically change your understanding of how much your brain influences reality and how much control you have over your reality and whether it is possible to manifest a new reality. Knowing this will also help you to change limiting beliefs and negative perceptions that could potentially inhibit your ability to manifest.

Before I explain how neuroscientists think the top-down version of events works I want you to try a thought experiment that I first encountered in *Being You*, written by neuroscientist Anil Seth. This thought experiment really helps to get your head around the top-down approach. Seth begins with the description of a scene from his life, so I will begin with one from mine; you can use my morning scene below or describe the scene that you are currently perceiving. If you choose your own, make sure to engage your senses and notice what you see, hear, feel, smell and taste.

I am lying on my stomach in bed, I stretch my hands under the pillow and enjoy the feel of the cool smooth cotton. I open my eyes and, with my head turned towards the edge of the bed, I see the corner of my pillow. Beyond that I see my bedside table with a bottle of sparkling water and my phone plugged into its charger. A little further in the distance I see my bedroom window and beyond that the trees in my garden with rooks and ravens on top, I see the grey sky, notice the chill in the air and the scent of the diffuser in my room. I hear the radiator rattle to life as the heating timer kicks in. I hear a toilet flush in the bathroom on the floor below, followed by the inevitable barking of my dogs, awakened by the old plumbing and eager for their morning walk. My mouth is dry, so I reach for the bottle of water.

Just like the bustling city of London with its intricate transport network keeping everything running smoothly, the jelly-like brain nestled within my skull orchestrates billions of interconnected neurons, each playing its unique part in the perception of my morning scene. Like trains racing through underground tunnels, sensory stimuli like the feel of cotton sheets, the scent of a diffuser or the sound of a toilet flushing trigger the electrical signals we call action potentials. These signals travel along neuronal branches and cross synapses like commuters navigating busy city stations.

Every perception, thought, feeling and action that I described is made possible by electro-chemical signalling. When I reach out to grasp my water bottle, there is increased activity in the brain areas that generate that movement. To feed this demand, oxygen is delivered to that area by my blood. Electrical signalling gives the brain its speed and the chemical transmission that occurs at the synapse gives the brain its flexibility. Neuronal transmission needs to happen at high speed, like a bullet train. Glial cells are a particular type of cell that wrap themselves around the cable-like communication branches in the brain, formulating an insulation sheath that facilitates speedy electrical conduction.

Take a moment. Close your eyes
Imagine that you are a brain
Place yourself inside the skull
It's a dark and silent place
There is no light. There is no sound

Fig. 5: Brain imagination activity

As you imagine being a brain, remember that in the dark, sound-less realm of the brain the incoming flow of electrical signals is ambiguous. There is no identifier to say that this signal is from a pillow and that one is from a bedside table. There isn't even an identifier to distinguish visual signals from sound signals or other types of sensory signals. So how does this deaf, blind, unfeeling brain turn these ambiguous sensory signals into my morning experience?

You might be surprised to learn that there is a lot of guesswork involved. You might also be surprised to learn that we perceive the world not as it actually is but in a way that best serves our purposes and needs. The brain uses predictions and best guesses to build our experience of an external world, a world that the brain can never directly encounter. This top-down view is entirely consistent with the data used to support the bottom-up view. One crucial aspect of the workings of the visual system is that the information doesn't just flow in one direction. The upper levels of the visual system hierarchy don't just receive information from lower levels of the visual system, they also send information back down to lower levels in a constant neural loop.

The way the brain harnesses these top-down connections to actively construct our perception of the outside world and shape what we experience is a form of predictive processing that is particularly useful for solving inverse problems.[5] Higher levels provide information about the type of things we might encounter and the range of hypotheses we might consider in any given situation.

Continuing the city government analogy, your brain is a city government that's trying to understand what's happening in the

---

5 An inverse problem in science is the process of calculating from a set of observations, data or knowns, the causal factors that produced the observations/data/knowns.

world outside its city hall. Because it's stuck in the city hall with no windows, it can't directly see or interact with the world outside. It relies on messages and reports from its different departments (the sensory inputs) to build a picture of what's happening outside. In this city government, information doesn't just flow in one direction, from the outside world to the government. It's a two-way street.

For example, let's consider the departments that handle visual information. In the previous analogy, we imagined that the lower-level departments are closer to the entrance and deal with basic, raw information about the external world. The higher-level departments are further in and deal with more complex information. The lower-level departments pass their reports up to the higher-level departments, but the higher-level departments also send their own reports back down to the lower levels. The higher-level parts of the brain use knowledge from past experiences to interpret current sensory data. When processing visual information, these brain areas, unrelated directly to vision, work with lower-level departments to form predictions and fill in any gaps. For example, if the lower-level reports something small and furry, the higher-level might guess it's a cat and adjust the understanding accordingly. This two-way exchange, called predictive processing, helps the brain construct a coherent view of the world. It's an essential tool that enables the brain to efficiently navigate our complex environment.

The brain's process of using predictions and best guesses to construct our experience of the external world relates to the practice of manifesting in several ways. Manifesting often involves visualising and imagining desired outcomes, which can be seen as the brain's attempt to generate predictions or mental representations of the desired reality. By creating a clear mental image of what we want to manifest, we are providing the brain with a specific goal or hypothesis to work towards.

The idea of top-down processing, where higher-level information influences the interpretation of lower-level sensory inputs, can also be applied to manifesting. When we engage in the practice of manifesting, we are consciously directing our attention towards positive thoughts, emotions and beliefs. These higher-level cognitive processes can shape the way we perceive and interpret our experiences, potentially influencing our actions and behaviours in alignment with our desired outcome.

The concept of predictive processing, where the brain's higher-level knowledge and predictions shape understanding of raw sensory data, can be related to the process of manifesting as well. By consistently focusing on our desired outcomes and maintaining a positive attitude, we are effectively providing the brain with a set of predictions or expectations. This can influence our perception of the external world and potentially guide our actions and choices in a way that supports the manifestation of our goals.

Just as the city government uses its strategists' predictions to interpret reports from the outside world, individuals practising manifesting can use their positive expectations and beliefs to interpret their experiences in a way that reinforces their desired outcomes. This constant exchange of information between higher-level cognition and sensory inputs helps shape our understanding of reality and can contribute to the manifestation of our goals.

In summary, the brain's predictive processing, top-down influence and the constant exchange of information between different levels of processing can be seen as underlying mechanisms that relate to the practice of manifesting. By consciously directing clear thoughts, emotions and beliefs towards our desired outcomes in a coherent way, we engage in a process that aligns our cognitive processing with the manifestation of our goals.

Human brains have evolved to predict as much as possible,

using information from our various senses to course-correct when the predictions don't work out. Rather than projecting an image onto the brain, the incoming sensory information serves as a form of error correction for the brain's best guess. The brain generates stories that are influenced and informed by our life experience. These stories are corrected, when necessary, by incoming signals.

Your brain acts like a prediction machine. It's always trying to guess what will happen next based on the sensory signals that bombard it. When I am looking at the bottle of water on my bedside locker, my brain is making educated guesses about the cause of the sensory signals originating from the bottle – shape, colour, texture, etc. A prediction error occurs when your brain's best guess doesn't match with the incoming sensory signal. These prediction errors register the difference between what your brain expects and what it gets at every level of processing. Your brain constantly works to minimise these by adjusting its predictions to better match the actual sensory information. Perception happens through a continuous process of minimisation of prediction error. Adjusting top-down predictions to eliminate bottom-up prediction errors keeps the stories that the brain generates about reality bound to their external causes. This is a critical point in the context of manifesting. Yes, neuroscience shows that your brain creates reality, but this created reality is always firmly tethered to the causes of the sensory signals. Your brain is not just making stuff up – it's interpreting and predicting based on real sensory information. It is scientifically possible to manifest your reality, but it would indeed be magic (or, more accurately, psychotic) if you manifested a reality that bears no relation to the outside world.

My subjective experience of seeing my water bottle on the locker is determined by the top-down predictions and not by the bottom-up sensory signals, which we never experience directly. My morning experience is an inside-out, top-down invention reined in by bottom-up sensory signals rather than a film reflecting reality. The entirety of perceptual experience is a neuronal invention tethered to the world outside your brain by a continuous making and remaking of perceptual best guesses informed by prediction errors. Still with me?

Our brain engages in guesswork to piece together our perceptions of the world. We all regularly experience instances where our brain guesses incorrectly. Only yesterday my husband's brain got it wrong when he mistook a pair of sand-coloured rocks for our dog, Dizzy. We were working in the garden clearing a lake-side path of debris after flooding. While David went to offload a trailer-load of debris, I rolled two large sand-coloured rocks over the path onto the edge of the grass. When David returned, his brain noticed something different – the outline of a new 'blond' shape at my feet – and made a best guess that it was our blond dog, as this would be a very likely scenario. As he got closer to me his brain took account of the more detailed information available at closer quarters and readjusted his perception from dog to rocks. I'm sure you've had similar illusions, perhaps mistaking a hoodie hanging on a door for a person or a black handbag on a chair for a cat or a hat. Our perceptual experience is a neural creation, a story composed by the brain – not an entirely fictitious story but one that is tied to the physical world through continuous making and refining of the brain's best guesses.

What we 'see' is not always an accurate reflection of the physical world. What we experience is a story generated by our brains. Our brains shape our perception of reality to meet our expectations or desires.

Are your brain's best guesses about yourself holding you back? Imagine Emily, an accomplished academic scientist. Despite her research achievements and published papers, she's haunted by the notion that she's an imposter, undeserving of her accolades. This imposter syndrome manifests as a constant inner critic that magnifies her flaws and minimises her achievements. When she walks into a conference room to present her ground-breaking research, her brain is already working overtime. To Emily, the room doesn't just hold an audience of her peers; it's more like an exam or even a courtroom, and she's the one on trial. Operating under the influence of limiting beliefs, her brain distorts the reality of the situation. It takes every crossed arm as a sign of scepticism, every unsmiling face as a mark of disapproval and every note scribbled as criticism waiting to be unleashed.

In reality, the crossed arms could be due to chilly air conditioning, the unsmiling faces may be absorbed in thought and the notes could be from peers impressed by her work, jotting down ideas her research has sparked. However, Emily's brain, primed by her limiting beliefs, fills in the gaps in a way that confirms her deepest fears. Her perception of reality is like a jigsaw puzzle. However, some pieces are shaped by past experiences, moulded by self-criticism and coloured in negative hues by her brain. She's solving the puzzle with pieces that don't quite fit, making the picture she completes far from what is actually in front of her. Emily's brain weaves a narrative that reinforces her limiting beliefs, even when external evidence might suggest otherwise. Her skewed perception doesn't just distort her current reality; it becomes a self-fulfilling prophecy that could affect her future interactions and opportunities impacting on her ability to manifest. In sum, our brains are masterful storytellers, but they can sometimes get the genre horribly wrong, turning what could be an empowering documentary into a disater movie, merely based on the scripts we've written for ourselves.

Signals from our senses are often very noisy. Noisy signals are full of superfluous information that needs filtering to reveal the useful bits. Essentially, noisy signals are distorted data or waveforms littered with random variations or unwanted changes. Imagine trying to measure the temperature outside your house, and random factors like gusts of wind, a barbeque or thermometer glitches disrupt the readings.

Given that our senses only capture a fraction of our environment, they rely on pooling information from all senses to guess the cause of a noisy signal. This is tough, as multiple potential causes exist and sometimes we lack enough information to trace the cause. In these instances, the brain taps into other knowledge or experiences to make a guess. For example, in the case of a visual stimulus, the brain will draw on additional information from other sources such as lighting, shading, texture, position or differences in the information received by each eye.

Let's take light and shade as examples. When we look at objects, our brains use light and shadow as cues to understand the objects' three-dimensional forms. What do you see if you look at the image below?

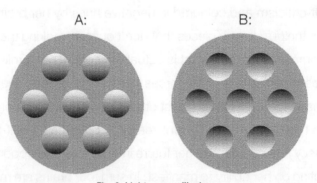

Fig. 6: Light source illusion

If you see convex bumps in image A and a series of concave depressions in image B, you are seeing what most people see. Now rotate this page and watch the bumps become depressions, and the depressions become bumps. Why?

This illusion illustrates how your brain uses prior knowledge of usual patterns of light and shade to make a best guess. Since light usually comes from above, your brain expects light from above and interprets the lighter parts as bumps or depressions depending on the orientation of the light and shade on the circles.

To create this illusion, I duplicated image A, turned it upside down and called it image B. After rotation, the lighter parts are at the bottom in a position that is consistent with shadows cast by dips rather than bumps when the source of light is above. This illusion is a really useful way to illustrate how systems in the brain have the ability to infer sensory stimuli from predictions that are the result of internal representations built through previous experience. The brain loves patterns and regularities because they facilitate prediction. Light from the sun comes from above and causes shadows to fall in particular patterns. These regularities allow the brain to build models of the world and make perceptual inferences.

The visual system, the most studied of our senses, operates in a top-down manner where information from upper hierarchy levels also travels downwards, supporting our ability to solve inverse problems. For example, during uncertain moments, like my husband mistaking rocks for our dog, information from the upper levels can suggest patterns or regularities to consider.

The dependability of sensory information is a critical factor in our perception. As the brain gathers more and more detailed information, the reliability of sensory input increases.

When faced with uncertain situations, our brains depend on reliable sensory information to update and refine their best guesses. Initially, a range of possibilities is considered, but as more informative cues become available the brain's inferences become more accurate and converge towards the most likely explanation. As you go about your day, your brain is constantly using past experiences and current possibilities to produce new perceptual best guesses every fraction of a second. Our perception is more like a lifelong rolling film than a millisecond snapshot. This means that the contents of our conscious experience are not just shaped by our brain's perceptual predictions, they *are* the perceptual predictions.

The concept of manifesting suggests that by focusing our thoughts and intentions we can shape our perception of the world and, to some extent, our experiences within it. This doesn't mean we can change the physical world with our thoughts – we can't think a chair or a million pounds into existence. But our thoughts and beliefs can influence our actions, decisions and interpretations of events, which can in turn affect our experiences and outcomes. In a sense, manifesting is like directing the movie of your perception.

If you're focused on positive thoughts and outcomes, your predictions or interpretations of the world might lean more towards seeing opportunities, success and positivity. You're more likely to take actions that align with these beliefs, leading to experiences that reflect them. This doesn't guarantee that everything will always go your way – there are many factors in life we can't control. But by shaping your perceptions and actions, manifesting could potentially influence your personal experiences and your overall outlook on life. In the grand scheme of things, this aligns with the understanding that our brains are continually updating and refining their interpretations of the world based on new sensory information. If the new information we focus on (our thoughts, beliefs and intentions) is positive and goal-oriented, it could influence our perception and experience of reality.

In summary, your brain is continually generating guesses about what you see, hear, smell and feel (perceptual predictions). It then checks these guesses against what the signals from your senses say. If your brain's guesses don't match these signals, your brain detects the mistake (prediction error) and adjusts the guess. Perceptual predictions (guesses) come from inside your brain (top-down) and prediction errors (mistakes) travel from the outside world into your brain (bottom-up). What you actually experience or perceive is a combination of all these brain guesses, but only after your brain has done its best to fix any mistakes it made. This means your perception is an educated guess made by your brain, based on your past experiences and the information it gets from your senses.

I should point out that prediction in 'prediction error' doesn't necessarily mean predicting the future; rather it means using a model to go beyond the data. Predictive processing theory doesn't just explain how the brain accomplishes perception, it also applies to cognition and action. The more information your brain has the better its predictions, and the more novel experiences you give your brain the better its predictions because you are collecting new information.

The final element of prediction error minimisation – precision weighting – has particular relevance for manifesting. In addition to figuring out the most likely cause of incoming signals, your brain also needs to assess how reliable the incoming signal is. Precision weighting allows the brain to adjust the influence of sensory signals on its best guesses. We do this all the time in everyday life. For example, imagine you are planning a holiday and you want to book a hotel in a city you've never visited before. You've come across three sources of information: a reputable travel agent you have used before, an anonymous online review and a recommendation from a close friend who regularly travels to this city. In this case precision weighting involves giving higher weight to the travel agent as they know their stuff and you have been happy with their recommendations in the past. You can't be certain that the anonymous review is credible or accurate so you would give it a lesser weighting. You trust your friend and you know you have similar tastes and standards, so you give their recommendation a significant weighting. Essentially, you prioritise the most reliable resources (agent and friend) and treat the online review with caution. From this you can make a more informed decision; you might even hit the jackpot in terms of making an easy decision if the agent and your close friend recommend the same hotel.

When your brain 'down-weights' a sensory signal (e.g. viewing something at a distance without your glasses) the signal will have less influence on updating the brain's best guess, and 'up-weighting' a signal (e.g. viewing something at closer range with glasses on) will have more influence. One way that we can increase estimated precision is by paying attention. When we focus our attention on something, let's say actively trying to figure out what a thing in the distance is, our brains increase the precision weighting of the corresponding incoming signals, enhancing their estimated reliability. When we focus our attention on specific sensory data, other data will have less influence on updating our best guesses. In some instances, unattended data will have no influence at all, resulting in what we call inattentional blindness (see Chapter Four).

In the context of manifesting, consider your thoughts, beliefs and intentions as sensory signals or information that your brain processes. The concept of manifesting emphasises the importance of focusing on these signals with positive and goal-oriented content. When it comes to precision weighting, the process could be seen as similar to deciding how much importance to give to these positive thoughts and intentions. If your brain perceives these thoughts as reliable or important (because you're focusing on them consistently and strongly), it could assign them a high weight. This could then influence your perception and interpretation of the world, making you more attuned to opportunities that align with your intentions, and more likely to take actions that help you achieve your goals. It's important to note that this doesn't mean thinking positively will instantly materialise your desires. However, by assigning high importance to positive and goal-oriented thoughts, you're essentially training your brain to prioritise these perspectives. This could attune your attention to opportunities, and keep you more focused on your goals, and more proactive in taking steps to achieve them.

Control

Action and perception are two sides of the same coin. Both rely on the minimisation of sensory prediction errors. Now that you've got your head around how the brain uses prediction to do this, it's time to see how action can be used to minimise sensory prediction errors. We can take action to change sensory information so that the new sensory data matches an existing prediction. Sounds a bit like cheating, I know, but here's how it works.

Active inference is the idea put forward by neuroscientist Karl Friston that the brain not only predicts what it will sense, but also takes actions to make those predictions come true. This, I think, is of particular interest in terms of manifesting because it means that your brain doesn't just passively receive information from the environment, but also actively tries to control it. Active inference has been described as a self-fulfilling perceptual prediction because it describes a process whereby the brain takes action to seek sensory data that makes its perceptual prediction come true. In other words, your brain uses action to make its predictions come true. Sounds a lot like manifesting, doesn't it? Predicting a future and then taking action to make it come true.

Here's how it works using a small everyday action like moving your eyes to change sensory data to match the brain's prediction. I am writing this in my garden on one of the first sunny days of May. My dogs can get very demanding of my attention when they are pent up in the house, disrupting my concentration when I am trying to write. In contrast, they tend to amuse themselves in the garden if I write outside. Every now and then I look up to check that my fourteen-year-old dog, Scruffy, a miniature Yorkie, hasn't wandered off as he is prone to do. I just looked up now and he wasn't where my brain predicted he would be based on his last position. To minimise this prediction error I move my eyes to scan other parts of the garden. As I scan the scene in front of me, the moment-to-moment visual predictions are being updated (bush, tree, hedge, sun lounger, pathway…). In addition, my visual focus is probing the scene until the perceptual prediction of Scruffy is fulfilled when my eyes find him lying in the shade of my sun lounger. My brain predicted that Scruffy was in the garden, and through the action of moving my eyes that prediction came true.

Any action of your body will change sensory data, whether it's looking over your shoulder, riding an escalator, walking out of your front room or pulling your shoulders back to stand taller. Any kind of action has the potential to quell sensory prediction errors through the process of active inference. Active inference relies on generative modelling, which is a concept that relates to the brain's ability to imagine, create and simulate experiences internally (aka visualisation). Just as artificial intelligence can generate new content based on patterns they've learned, our brain has the extraordinary capacity to generate mental representations (e.g. visualisations), scenarios and simulations based on past experiences. This generative process allows us to imagine future possibilities, explore creative ideas and imagine different outcomes, enhancing our cognitive flexibility and creativity. Active inference specifically relies on the ability of generative models to predict the sensory consequences of actions. Essentially, it is about using our past experiences to estimate what we might experience through our senses when we take an action.

For example, if I look over my shoulder what sensory data am I likely to encounter? This is called a conditional prediction because it deals with what would happen if something were to be the case. These conditional predictions help the brain to know which action among multiple possible actions is most likely to reduce sensory prediction errors. In my Scruffy example my brain predicted that visually scanning the garden, rather than calling Scruffy (he has gone quite deaf), was the action most likely to find my dog.

Active inference also applies to high-level actions like applying for a new job, buying a house or getting married because these actions are the result of multiple sets of bodily actions that alter sensory input. I've made it clear from the outset that manifesting requires action. Whether your manifesting goal is to get a new job, a new husband or a more optimistic outlook on life, your manifesting journey will be made up of smaller physical actions that alter sensory inputs, changing what we see, hear and feel. Every action, no matter how small, has the power to reshape your perception of the world. This is because each action we take helps to narrow the gap between what we predict will happen and what actually happens; this is the essence of active inference. Every action we take is a key player in shaping our perception and our reality. The most counterintuitive aspect of active inference – that the actions themselves are self-fulfilling perceptual predictions – is also the aspect that is echoed in the pervasive 'act as if' (aka 'fake it till you make it') technique in manifesting, i.e. you act as if you already are who you want to be.

Your body has its own built-in GPS system called proprioception that constantly tracks the position and movement of your limbs and other parts of your body. Whether you are dancing, playing soccer, or, like me now, typing words on my laptop, proprioception is a form of perception, an unsung hero making it all happen seamlessly, under the radar. Proprioception registers sensory signals that flow from receptors in your skeleton and muscles to keep track of where your body is and how it is moving. I have just taken a sip of water from the glass on the table beside me. When we talk about active inference, taking a sip from my water glass involves my brain making a prediction about where my body is, where the glass is, and how I should move to drink from it. This prediction is so strong that it overrides what I'm actually sensing, like feeling my hands on my laptop's keyboard or knowing the glass is on the coffee table next to me. Essentially, my brain expects the action to happen and acts in a way to make it a reality. I know this sounds a bit mad, but bear with me; here's how it works . . .

For the proprioceptive prediction to come true, the prediction errors that signal the brain where my body actually is must be down-weighted. This lack of focused attention on where my body is allows my body to move. Again this is echoed in a technique we see in manifesting where people are discouraged from paying attention to what they don't want so that they can take action and make progress towards what they want to manifest. Thinking about action in this way negates the need for 'the mind' as middleman because action and perception are both forms of brain-based prediction that rely on best-guessing. What all of this means is that we perceive our top-down predictions. Our reality is simply our brain's best guess of the causes of sensory inputs.

Novelty

Active inference is like gathering more clues and information so that your brain gets better and better at making predictions. Active inference helps the brain make better guesses about what's going to happen next. It's a way for your brain to improve its ability to anticipate and understand what's going on in the world around you. Over short periods, our actions can gather new sensory data that can help to improve best guesses or decide between competing perceptual options. In the heel of the hunt, actions are fundamental to learning. Actions improve the brain's generative models because they provide new sensory data about the causes of specific sensory signals and about causal processes in the world in general.

Many manifesting coaches say, in one way or another, that manifesting is about the journey not the destination. The destination is your overall manifesting goal, but change, learning and satisfaction come from the actions you take on the journey to the goal. Have you noticed that after the initial euphoria of reaching a goal, which you believe will make you happy, you often feel flat? Attaining the result you wished for is not the endgame for your brain. This is because your brain needs new experiences and ongoing challenges to learn from the world and make ever more accurate predictions. It is not the end result or the outcome that brings us happiness or contentment; it is the journey, the learning, the evolution, the setting of new goals. These are the things that activate the reward, pleasure and motivation centres in our brains. These are the things that produce feelings of pleasure, reward, satisfaction and motivation. These are the things that provide opportunities for flow, all because your brain hungers for knowledge to refine its best guesses and ultimately to maintain homeostasis and ensure your survival.

You now know that the brain needs to make predictions to navigate the world and to manifest great things. The more information your brain has about your environment the better able it is to compare environments and experiences and predict the possibility of certain outcomes. The brain makes inferences using incoming sensory information combined with expectations based on experience and new sensory information gleaned from our actions.

Change, doing new things, having new experiences provides your brain with more data, allowing it to update internal models of the environment and make more accurate predictions about the world. For example, in a relatively short period of time though trial and error you learn the force you need to assert when opening or closing the door to the garden in your new home. One night during a storm you apply the same force when opening the door and are taken by surprise when the door flies out of your hand with the force of the wind. This experience is new data, which your brain can draw on in the future to make better predictions, thus minimising uncertainty and errors. Next time there is a storm, incoming sensory information (howling wind) combined with your past experience (door flying out of your hand) improves the accuracy of your brain's prediction and your behaviour is adjusted so that you apply greater force to hold onto the door or decide not to open the door at all.

Many things in our environment behave in predictable ways; an empty cup will always feel lighter than a full cup, your back door will be more likely to slam when there is a wind than when there is not, your eldest son will always avoid washing the dishes unless he wants something. When your brain takes advantage of the predictable structure of incoming sensory information, fewer attentional resources are required. This means that your brain doesn't have to process and remember every sound, image, smell, etc. that you encounter in every moment. Prediction is an efficient use of limited neural resources that serves us well, allowing us to adapt to our ever-changing environment. This adaptability, this neuroplasticity is what underlies resilience. When you resist change you deny your brain important data and reduce its predictive power. You also deny yourself the opportunity to build resilience and experience happiness. Manifesting promotes adaptability and resilience because it is all about change and change involves novelty.

Your brain thrives on predictability and this need for predictability drives your brain to seek novelty. It sounds counterintuitive, but essentially it just means that the more information your brain has the more accurate its predictions become. Casey loved the apple tart her mum used to make, which was the only apple tart she had ever tasted. When she started a job in a new area she saw an apple tart in a local coffee shop that looked just like her mum's. Combining this incoming sensory information with her past but limited experience of apple tart, her brain predicts that she will like it. On tasting it she discovered that this apple tart, tastes very different from the one her mum makes because this one is made with cloves. Casey dislikes cloves. Her brain now has new data (some apple tarts contain cloves) and will modify future predictions (I may not like this particular apple tart) and shape her behaviour accordingly (don't buy apple tart at my local coffee shop and check whether future apple tarts I encounter contain cloves).

The human brain is incredibly responsive to the environment. As you learned earlier, it has an amazing ability to adapt and change in response to personal, social and cultural experiences. It does this by reorganising itself and growing new connections between neurons. This flexibility, this neuroplasticity, describes how the brain changes as it assimilates new information.

Paradoxically, we have a natural tendency to resist change, in part because change requires effort and also because the unknown may contain threats or stressors. Your brain is built for change and thrives on challenge. Your brain is constantly changing and it's your behaviours, your experiences and the life choices that you make that shape it. Change requires effort but it is rewarding and with time becomes effortless. Embracing change on an ongoing basis is fundamental to happiness. This is because the human brain is adaptable. This ability at the core of resilience allows us to cope and grow with challenge. It also means that we adapt to the things that bring us happiness, we get used to them and so we must seek out new challenges and welcome change on an ongoing basis to attain ongoing happiness. The goal that you are striving to manifest now is just one in an ongoing, ever-changing cycle of working towards and attaining multiple goals in sequence or in parallel.

Change

At the highest level, manifesting is about change, about taking action to attain your goals and change your life for the better. You have been changing all your life, constantly moving from one state or situation to another. Sometimes life throws you a curveball and change is unexpected and unwelcome. This type of change can overwhelm us and lead to feelings of anxiety, depression, hurt, frustration, sadness, loss or regret. However, with the right tools this type of change can become an opportunity for growth, for building resilience and for personal, positive transformation. Manifesting is about choosing to change and the skills that you learn in that process will help you manage both expected and unexpected types of change that life will inevitably bring. Understanding the psychology and neuroscience of change is key to successful manifesting.

Change is hard work. No matter how much you want to change, welcome change, wish for change or will change to occur, bringing about change requires effort. There is no point pretending otherwise. While your brain is adaptable in the face of change, it doesn't like uncertainty and as a consequence resists change. Your brain will opt for the known, predictable outcome, over an uncertain one. Change is aversive because your brain can't anticipate the outcome. Your brain's main priority is to keep you alive and maintain a stable equilibrium (homeostasis) across all systems. Change threatens this status quo. In anticipation of threat your brain jumps into protective mode. Our inherent drive for survival prioritises predictability over uncertainty. Change challenges this and the fear response is activated; as a result we may fight change, run from it, or become frozen by the prospect of it. The anticipation of change activates the fear centres in the brain, clouding both our ability to think rationally and our ability to see our own potential. Paradoxically, our brain's inherent adaptability and flexibility means that we not only have the skills to change and evolve but welcoming change is critical in order for us to thrive, survive and be resilient in the face of adversity. Manifesting acts like a motivator for change and new experiences.

You won't be embarking on your manifesting journey with a clean slate. Most manifesting coaches acknowledge that you will likely need to change entrenched habits or everyday routines to achieve your manifesting goals, and that's hard work. Be careful not to change routines that work well for you though, that would be counter-productive. Starting from scratch would be so much easier, in the same way that building a new house from fresh plans is so much easier to do and control than renovating an old house where you have to account for and work with existing structures that may require remediation and upgrading. Research shows that deciding to change on or just after a fresh start can give the impression of a clean slate and act as a clean break from the past. Fresh starts can take many forms: a new year, a new semester, a birthday, after a holiday, etc. Manifesting represents an opportunity to kick-start change, it permits turning the clock back to zero, resetting your score or erasing your track record and starting anew.

All of the aspects of manifesting are interlinked and so it is difficult to write about change in isolation. Other topics discussed in later chapters will have relevance for attaining change; the choices that you make, the thoughts that you think, the emotions that you feel, the behaviour that you enact and indeed the behaviours that you don't enact will all play a role in your manifesting journey.

The key to successful change is understanding your opponent. Considering that most of the biggest barriers to change, such as procrastination, lack of self-confidence, pessimism, forgetfulness, laziness and impulsivity, are internal, it's safe to say that you are your greatest opponent. Never forget that successful change often takes several attempts. Having clarity about the changes that you want to make is a great first step.

CHAPTER FOUR
Clarity

*'In the pursuit of wisdom clarity is
the torch that lights the way'*
Unknown

Clarity

Clarity is often emphasised as a crucial step in the practice of manifesting. Clarity helps you home in on what you truly want, which is necessary for setting goals and maintaining the focus that manifestation requires. Without a clear vision, the energy and attention required for manifestation could become scattered, reducing the effectiveness of your efforts. In a way, clarity acts as a compass, guiding you towards your desired outcome. Several prominent authors have spoken about the importance of clarity in terms of what you want and who you are. Jack Canfield, author of *The Success Principles*, captured the fundamental importance of clarity to manifesting when he said, 'vague goals produce vague results'.

There is nothing hugely ground-breaking in the idea of being clear about what you want. It's something that we know from our day-to-day lives ensures success. Let's take food shopping, for example. Let's imagine you decide to do your food shopping with only a vague idea of what you want. If you head to the supermarket without checking what you already have and without taking time to figure out what you might like to eat every day, you are likely to return home with some things you don't need and without things you really needed. As a result you will have to make further trips to the supermarket or end up going hungry or having the same dinner a few nights to use up the duplicates. Now imagine the alternative where your goal is to stock up on ingredients for the week's meals. A clear vision of what you desire significantly increases your chances of success. You begin visualising what you would like to eat, you might take account of certain activities during the week and realise that you don't need to cook on Wednesday as you are meeting a friend for dinner. You might remember that you need to buy extra as you are having friends over for supper on Friday. You check the cupboards and fridge to see what you have and what you need in order to achieve your goal of purchasing what you need for the week. You then create a shopping list, which is a concrete reflection of your needs and desires.

Armed with this list, you enter the supermarket and systematic- ally select items off the shelves. You may be drawn to some other items, like a special offer, which could distract you or spark you to change your plans about what you will cook for your guests on Friday. Or you may also discover that certain items on your list that are key ingredients for Friday's supper are out of stock, presenting you with several options for responding to this unexpected turn of events. You could, of course, simply accept the unavailability and proceed without these items. Alternatively, you could pivot towards an alternate brand or alternate ingredient, remaining flexible in the face of the unexpected. If you're particularly determined, you might modify your original plan by venturing to a different supermarket in search of the elusive items. You might even explore several supermarkets. It's also possible that you might stumble upon the ingredient in the first, second or third store you visit. Let's consider a scenario where despite you trying all of the supermarkets in your locality your desired items remain persistently absent. In this case you might make an executive decision to revise your original plan and go for an entirely different menu for Friday night. You revisit and amend your list and actions accordingly.

In essence, your initial clarity of intent – the creation of a clear and specific shopping list – steers you towards successful action, accommodating adjustments along the way as needed. This is pretty much what happens throughout the manifesting process; beginning with taking stock of what you have, imagining in detail what you want in the near future, taking action to move you toward your goal and incorporating some revisions along the way in response to the unexpected.

People might refer to this approach as common sense. But rather interestingly it's not something that we always do, and so part of the reason why manifesting works is that it motivates people to apply the same principles that you would with effective supermarket shopping to attaining life goals and desires. It guides us through the process of gaining clarity about what we want, deciding on the actions we need to take, making revisions and ultimately attaining our goals with the possibility that we may discover other options along the way.

One of the first things I learned as a psychology undergraduate was not to trust common sense, particularly when trying to understand human behaviour. While our common-sense beliefs can be reasonably accurate, scientific research indicates that no matter how intuitive a belief feels there's a good chance it could be wrong. This made me curious to find out whether our common-sense feelings about clarity are supported by neuroscience.

On a day-to-day basis the human brain hasn't got the bandwidth to test common-sense beliefs or form detailed and accurate beliefs about everything, so it has to rely on heuristics. When a common-sense belief is widely shared, makes intuitive sense and is endorsed by experts we have a natural tendency to take a mental shortcut and assume that it is true. We also have a natural tendency to focus on instances that confirm our intuitive beliefs rather than those that contradict them. Rather than simply accepting the common sense that clarity is fundamental to manifesting, I want to delve a little deeper into the neuroscience, I want to understand why clarity matters to the brain. What difference does it make? What happens in your brain when you have clarity about that which you wish to manifest? Having a clear vision takes work. Visualising (see Chapter Six) your goals and desires is a very useful technique for gaining clarity. Manifesting generally involves extending this technique beyond the visual to include imagining how it would feel, which can give invaluable insight into whether your stated goal will actually bring about what you really, really want. Transforming the intellectual to the visceral in your imagination can help you to get to the core of what you truly desire. Paying attention to every functional and aesthetic detail is effortful and tedious, but essential for forward planning. Drawing up accurate plans is essential for a successful build. Understanding that you may have to compromise, adapt and revise those plans is also an important ingredient for success.

Manifesting generally begins with deciding on a desired outcome or result and working backward to identify the actions, beliefs and circumstances that can lead to its realisation. This process is similar to solving inverse problems, where you begin with the knowns (the desired outcome) and then determine the unknowns (the active steps you need to take to achieve it). This manifesting approach works because the human brain is a master at navigating uncertainty because of its incredible ability to solve inverse problems. Manifesting requires us to tap into this neural problem-solving ability to create the reality we desire.

The human brain has evolved to excel at finding solutions to inverse problems, in dynamic situations that involve stimuli from multiple senses. A pretty amazing feat considering our brains are confined inside a dark skull with only signals from our senses to work backwards from to determine the cause. When manifesting, we use our imagination and intentions as the knowns and then work backward to identify the actions, attitudes and opportunities needed to attain our desired outcome. We start with gaining clarity about what we want (the knowns) and then engage in a process of exploring and working backward to uncover the steps (the unknowns) that we need to take to bring about our manifesting goals.

Manifesting allows us to recognise and create opportunities in our lives by working backward from the desired outcome. By harnessing our brain's problem-solving abilities and using the knowns to uncover the unknowns, we can actively shape our reality and manifest our dreams.

Attention

Rhonda Byrne emphasises the power of thoughts and visualisation. According to Byrne, you can attract what you desire by focusing on it, believing you will receive it and visualising having it. She underscores the importance of positivity and gratitude in the process. I will discuss what neuroscience can tell us about how visualisation, positive thinking and gratitude work in Chapter Six. In this chapter, I explain the neuroscience behind our ability to attract what we desire. By the end of this chapter you will come to realise the empowering truth that, once you have clarity about what you want, focused attention rather than attraction is what drives success.

I've never paid much attention to cars; they're not my thing. I couldn't tell you what kind of car my neighbour drives, I barely know what kind of car my husband drives. I don't have aspirations about owning or manifesting a specific type of car. However, many years ago when my fiancé (now my husband) and I needed to dip into the savings for our house to buy a second-hand car, I paid attention because it mattered to me what we spent that hard-earned cash on. My husband, to whom cars matter, felt that we should buy a Mazda 323. A model of car that I never knew existed until my husband showed me an advert for a second-hand one in the newspaper (pre-internet). The next morning and every other morning for the following week I saw several Mazda 323s as I walked past traffic on my way to and from work. The number of Mazda 323s in my environment had not increased. I hadn't attracted them into my world nor had I magically manifested more Mazda 323s, but I was definitely seeing more of them. How?

The cars were always there, I just hadn't noticed them before. They were in my line of vision, but I didn't consciously perceive them. How is it possible not to see something that is right in front of you? This is possible because at a high level our perception of reality, of the world around us, is the result of an interaction between sensory data from the environment (the things we see, hear, touch, taste and smell) and internal cognitive processes including attention, expectation, memory and the brain's best-guess heuristics.

During sensation, our sensory organs convert one type of energy (e.g. light or sound waves) to another (electrical impulses) through a process called transduction. As you know, brain cells communicate using electrical and chemical signals and some brain cells specialise in responding to certain types of sensory stimuli. When the visual information from the environment – for example a red balloon floating over the rooftops – hits the eye's retina, the information is relayed to the visual cortex, which is located at the back of the brain. Different systems within the visual cortex process different aspects of the physical visual information, allowing us to see the shape (oval), colour (red), movement (floating) and location (over the rooftops) of the balloon.

Perception involves the interpretation, organisation and conscious experience of information taken in through any of our senses. In essence, the process of perceiving adds meaning to the physical information. This not only allows us to identify the moving object as a balloon, it allows us to put it in context and add meaning – 'oh no, that's my three-year-old's birthday balloon, she is going to be inconsolable'.

Incoming sensory data from the environment – the shape, the colour, the movement, the location – is the data upon which perceptions are built from the top down inside the brain. Our interpretation of the incoming visual information is influenced by our thinking, our prior knowledge, our life experiences, our motivations, our moods, our expectations and so much more. Not all sensations result in perceptions. What we pay attention to, our beliefs, our values, our prejudices, our culture and life experience don't just affect how we perceive something but whether we perceive something at all.

A dramatic experiment illustrates this really well. Researchers asked participants to watch a video of people passing a basketball and count the number of passes made by one of the teams. During the video, a person in a gorilla suit walked through the basketball game, paused to look at the camera, then beat his chest before walking off screen. Half of the people watching the video failed to notice the gorilla, who spent a total of nine seconds on screen. This experiment illustrates the phenomenon known as inattentional blindness brilliantly, showing how focusing on a specific thing can cause us to miss other significant information, even something as conspicuous as a person in a gorilla suit! It highlights really well how focusing on one thing can cause us to overlook other things, even if they are in plain sight.

Attention influences our perception of the world. What we focus on matters and can make or break our ability to manifest. For example, selectively focusing on the negatives in your life can, like focusing on counting the number of passes in the selective attention video, literally blind you to opportunity and to the positives in your life.

Attention is one of those things we talk about regularly but rarely define. From a scientific perspective, attention refers to a mental state where our cognitive resources focus on certain aspects of the environment over others and the central nervous system, which includes the brain, is alert and ready to respond. It is a very important brain function. Without this ability it would be impossible to get anything done or attain any goals. Our brain constantly scans the environment for various things that are salient to us; things that are currently significant or important to us, things that we will find rewarding as well as things that we are fearful of, things that threaten us or things that could cause us harm.

At the most fundamental level the human brain will prioritise information pertinent to keeping you alive, such as the speed, distance and trajectory of a car. Your brain also has capacity to pay attention to information that has meaning for you, so you will be able to pick out your spouse's car in a line of traffic while waiting on a lift, or notice your ex's car parked outside the restaurant you are about to enter with your new partner. Essentially, the human brain directs attention to things that have salience, things that matter to us, things that are important to us, things that have meaning for us. Things that we want to manifest.

Once I considered buying a Mazda 323 I started to notice them everywhere because my brain was directing my attention to them, not because I attracted them. The introspection and self-awareness required to gain clarity around your desires are a means to manifesting. Gaining clarity around these things is essentially a way to message your brain about what information is salient to you now, to attaining your goals.

The human brain, which consists of multiple, distinct and interacting networks, does not have infinite capacity and so it is not possible to attend to everything going on in our internal and external worlds. The 'salience network', located at the interface of cognitive, homeostatic, motivational and emotional systems in the brain, plays a critical role in picking out the most biologically and cognitively relevant stimuli from both internal and external sources.

The nervous system uses two saliency detection mechanisms in the brain to actively select specific stimuli from the constant stream of sensory information for further processing. The first is a fast automatic mechanism that filters sensory stimuli based on perceptual features (colour, size, shape, speed, etc.). Salience filters can enhance the response to things that are of instinctive biological importance (water, food, etc.), of learned significance (traffic lights), or that occur infrequently (a random loud noise) as they ascend the neural pathways to the sensory cortex in the brain and ultimately to our conscious experience.

The second mechanism is a system for focusing attention and enhancing access to the resources needed for directing behaviour towards goals. This 'salience network', a core brain system for stimulus selection in the midst of competing stimuli, will likely filter and amplify things that are salient to the self, emotionally engaging, pleasurable, rewarding, surprising and/or unusual. It's a bit like a spotlight for your brain, helping you concentrate on what's important and gather the necessary tools to guide your actions towards achieving your goals. This 'salience network' is a key part of the brain that helps you choose what to pay attention to when there are many things going on around you, highlighting positive things and things that are relevant to your manifesting goal. This keeps you goal-focused, positive and less aware of negatives and distractors.

Many factors influence this type of attention; for example, your past experience will influence what you perceive in the environment. You will experience this as noticing things that have meaning for you. For months after my father died, wherever I went I noticed older men with my dad's build, wearing flat caps, like the one my dad wore.

You also have some voluntary control over attention. For example, when you actively scan a car park looking for your car, study for an exam or read a book. Attention can also be captured involuntarily by things in your environment like a speeding car, the repeated pattern of a convoy of cars from a radio station, the contrast between a battered old wreck and a shiny new car or something that you have never seen before.

Let's take an everyday situation where your brain is bombarded by multiple stimuli through various senses, as you stand waiting to cross a busy road at a traffic light. There will be cars, of course, but there will also be other people, smells, sounds, temperature, the weather, the colour of the sky, the colour of the traffic lights – the amount of incoming information is phenomenal. The relative salience of these inputs determines which is most likely to capture my attention – the Mazda 323, the good-looking guy standing next to me, the man in the flat cap standing in front of me, the rumbling in my stomach, or the grey clouds that might spoil the barbeque I'm on my way to. The salience network plays a key role in detection of relevant stimuli and the coordination of neural resources. Key nodes of this network are located in a really well-connected part of the brain called the insular cortex. Incoming information is processed and evaluated here and predictions are made based on the incoming data, previous knowledge and experience.

It's practically impossible to get anything done without the capacity to selectively focus our attention on the things that are relevant to whatever we are doing at any point in time. Every second each eye receives about a hundred megabits of information (that's faster than my broadband). Your brain needs to categorise incoming information as relevant or irrelevant to the task at hand, or to your longer-term goals, to avoid being overwhelmed by the sensory information in the environment. Once you have clarity about what you want to manifest, your brain will direct your attention to information salient to manifesting what you desire. Having clarity about what you want to manifest is critical for success and a key way that manifesting works. Your brain needs to be clear about what you want in order to draw your attention to things that are relevant to that goal.

Being clear about what you want to manifest primes your brain to work towards that goal. Many manifesting processes involve some form of 'back-to-the-drawing-board' revision option to ensure that what you strive for is actually what you really want. Detailed visualising of how your new life or new you will look and feel is a way of trying it on for size. In the process of detailed imagining you may discover that what you dreamed about isn't actually a good fit or not really you, or who you want to be. Using visualisation to refine and return to the drawing board is a really effective way to gain clarity about what you really, really want.

What Do You Really, Really Want?

Life is not a problem to be solved, it is a gift of time, a journey to be enjoyed. Modern life can estrange us from our true nature and fool us into chasing success that feels meaningless, disconnected from our unique inner passion and joy and divorced from what we really want. It is easy to lose your way while your brain focuses on simply surviving or striving for success. It's a real struggle to think clearly or focus your attention when you feel like you're running on empty. When you feel overwhelmed by the busyness of day-to-day life you simply haven't got the headspace to consider your dreams, let alone follow them. Without clarity your brain can become overwhelmed by the barrage of incoming signals. Manifesting encourages the savouring of life's journey, offering an opportunity to calm the chaos and find clarity through the use of a selection of techniques (Chapter Six) that help you identify beliefs and patterns of thinking, behaving and feeling that have cluttered your brain and distanced you from the things that bring joy, purpose and meaning to your life. Visualisation, journaling, positive thinking and other tools can bring you greater clarity about what you really want and what you would truly like to manifest, rather than what you feel you should manifest, currently want to manifest and possibly even what you have been working towards manifesting for a long time. To manifest your dreams your brain needs a clear picture of what you want to manifest.

In the Western world it is so easy to fall victim to the societal swindle that sells money, power, success and all that goes with it as rewarding, sure-fire routes to happiness. Connecting with your internal compass can direct you to your inner passion to give your life meaning and purpose, two things that are often at the core of what people deep down really want from life. By tagging your passion as important your brain will filter information to focus your attention on what is salient to your personal passion. As a consequence, you will notice opportunities to hone that passion and, if it is what you really wish to manifest, your brain will direct you to opportunities to do what you love in life.

Doctor Wayne Dyer, a renowned self-help author and motivational speaker, emphasised the importance of having a clear vision in the process of manifesting. He believed that being clear about what you want and need in your life will help you 'be' and allow those things to manifest. When you engage in something that you love doing you lose yourself completely in the act of doing. Paradoxically, this is where you find yourself and can just be; you have let go of the observer within. You become fully present in the moment, focused on what you are doing while you are doing it. Your deep involvement with the activity at hand removes awareness of worries and stresses, distancing you from anxiety and depression. You are at one with yourself. Your sense of time is altered, hours can seem like minutes. Your concentration is so absolute that it can be difficult for external events like your partner calling you to dinner and internal signals like hunger to break the joyous spell. You are 'in the zone', you have entered a 'flow' state.

There have been relatively few studies into this kind of human experience, which is often referred to as 'flow'. The concept of flow, coined by psychologist Mihaly Csikszentmihalyi, describes a mental state in which a person becomes fully immersed and engaged in an activity, experiencing a sense of energised focus, enjoyment and the loss of self-consciousness. Flow is a phenomenon that is frequently achieved by athletes, artists and scientists who manifest peak performance. But it is also commonly experienced in more mundane work and leisure activities, like writing a report to a deadline, decorating your home or completing multiple levels of a console game without feeling bored, fatigued or hungry. It is accompanied by feelings of accomplishment, meaningfulness, positive mood and a sense of wellbeing. Identifying your passion will not only help bring clarity about what you want to manifest, it will bring pleasure, purpose and positivity to your life.

The concept of flow, or 'being in the zone', is likely linked to manifesting or achieving personal and professional goals in a few ways. Flow increases focus. When you're in a state of flow, your concentration is fully dedicated to the task at hand. This deep level of focus allows you to make significant progress and often leads to higher-quality results. For manifestation, this level of focus can be particularly valuable because it enables you to connect with your true passion, envision your goals with clarity and think about the steps required to achieve them.

Flow enhances performance. Flow state is often associated with optimal performance. You are more creative, efficient and productive when you're in this state. This can help you achieve more in less time, bringing you closer to your manifesting objectives.

Flow improves learning and skill development. Being in the flow can also enhance your capacity to learn and improve. This is critical for personal growth and skill development, the kind of change required to successfully manifest.

Flow increases pleasure and enjoyment. Flow can make the process of working towards your goals more enjoyable. This can increase your intrinsic motivation, the motivation that comes from internal rewards. Being in the flow can make you feel energised. When you enjoy the process of working towards your goal, you're more likely to stick with it. Flow is associated with feeling optimistic and positive, making it more likely that we feel compassion towards ourselves.

Flow supports coherence. To successfully manifest, it's often recommended to not only visualise your end goal, but to also align your emotional and mental state with the feeling of having already achieved your goal. The positive state associated with being in flow can help create this alignment.

Flow reduces anxiety and stress. Flow involves a sense of effortlessness and ease, which can counter feelings of anxiety and stress. This creates a more positive mental environment conducive to manifestation. When you are fully present there is no room for self-criticism and it is not possible to worry or be depressed about the future or the past.

There is still a lot to learn, but we do know that the dopaminergic system, the area of our brain involved in reward, is more active during the experience of flow and corresponds with feeling optimistic, positive, energised and motivated, facilitating the deep focus, enjoyment and intrinsic motivation associated with flow.

In summary, achieving a state of flow can be a powerful way to support the process of manifestation. By encouraging deep focus, enhancing performance, increasing enjoyment and promoting a positive mental state, flow can help bring your manifesting goals into reality.

From a neuroscience perspective, research on the state of flow is still evolving, but there are several hypotheses and studies that try to explain this phenomenon. One common theory is that during flow, the prefrontal cortex – the area of the brain responsible for self-reflective consciousness, self-monitoring and impulse control – exhibits temporary slowing of activity, known in scientific lingo as transient hypo frontality. This reduction in activity may contribute to the loss of self-consciousness and time distortion often reported during flow.

Think of your brain as a busy city again, with messages constantly being passed around. Just like in a city, there are various ways these messages – neurotransmitters, hormones and cytokines – can be delivered. Neurotransmitters are like the local mail service. They deliver messages really quickly across small distances – from just one brain cell (neuron) to the next one. An example is dopamine, a neurotransmitter that helps pass along messages about things like pleasure and reward, kind of like a 'Good news!' postcard sent from one neuron to another.

Hormones are more like express courier packages sent across the whole city. They're made in certain areas of the brain and body and travel in the bloodstream to deliver specific messages to particular parts of the brain. They usually work more slowly than neurotransmitters, but their effects are typically longer lasting. For example, cortisol is a hormone that the body releases when it's stressed, kind of like an 'Urgent: Act Now!' courier package that helps to get various parts of your body on the same page and ready to react to a stressful situation by increasing glucose in the bloodstream, enhancing the brain's use of glucose and increasing the availability of substances that repair tissue. It also curbs or alters functions not essential to the fight or flight response, suppressing the digestive system, the reproductive system and growth processes and altering immune system responses.

Cytokines are a bit like emergency broadcast announcements in the city, usually linked to how your body responds to things like injuries or infections. These are proteins made by cells in your immune system, and they help send signals to control your body's immune response. Interleukin-1 (IL-1), for example, is a cytokine that sends out an 'Attention! We need help here!' signal when there's an injury or infection, helping to kick-start your body's defence system. Your brain is constantly buzzing with these chemical messages, all working together to help keep things running smoothly. The state of flow has been associated with the release of several neurochemicals, including dopamine, which enhances the brain's ability to process information and heightens attention, pattern recognition and motivation.

Recent brain studies have given us some insights into flow – the mental state where everything seems to click and tasks feel effortless. The research suggests that flow happens when two networks in the brain – the default mode network (DMN) and the task positive network (TPN) – find a perfect balance. You may recall that the DMN is activated when we daydream, visualise and think about ourselves. The TPN takes care of goal-driven tasks. During flow, these normally opposing networks start working together in harmony.

Imagine your brain as a vast network of highways, with different routes responsible for different mental states. In the case of flow, the DMN and the TPN are the two main routes that come into play. The DMN is like a scenic route, associated with imagining, daydreaming and self-reflection. In contrast, the TPN is like an efficient expressway, activated when we're engaged in goal-oriented activities and focused on a particular task.

During flow, something fascinating happens on this mental highway system. Neuroimaging studies suggest that the activation of the DMN and TPN, which are typically inversely related (like two roads going in opposite directions), may actually become positively correlated, like two roads flowing in the same direction. This positive correlation between the DMN and TPN during flow indicates a unique harmony in the brain. It suggests that, in this state, our daydreaming tendencies blend seamlessly with our ability to stay focused and achieve goals. It's like experiencing the best of both worlds, where our brain effortlessly navigates between introspection and laser-like concentration. During flow, it's as if the scenic route and the motorway align perfectly, creating a mental state where our thoughts flow effortlessly, our focus is razor-sharp, and we achieve a harmonious balance between self-reflection and goal-directed action.

Some research suggests that brainwave activity shifts during flow, showing an increase in alpha and theta brainwaves, patterns typically associated with relaxation and creativity. Neuroscience's understanding of flow is still emerging and many of these theories are based on indirect evidence or are still being refined and tested. Having said that, it is not unreasonable to suggest that the practices associated with manifesting increase the likelihood of accessing the flow state.

Finding your passion requires matching your skills to the activity or task that you engage in. If the task is too easy it won't engross you and you will become bored. If the task is too difficult, beyond your skills, then you will experience frustration or stress. When both are aligned, you achieve coherence, a perfect match, you connect to your personal sweet spot, you are fully engaged; this is the essence of flow.

Discovering your passion often begins with understanding your skills and talents. Reflecting on what you enjoy and where your natural abilities lie can help to guide this process. This self-awareness is, as you know, a foundational step in manifestation. You need to know what you truly desire to begin the process of bringing it into your reality. When you find something that hits the sweet spot between your skills and a meaningful challenge, you're more likely to enter a state of flow. This balance can keep you engaged and passionate about what you're doing, which is critical for sustained effort towards manifesting your goals. When you experience flow and working with passion, it becomes easier to visualise and manifest your goals. Being fully engaged in what you're doing brings a clarity of purpose that can help make your manifestation more specific and tangible. Flow is transient, but, once you have identified your passion and how to engage it, you can aim to create the conditions that allow you to more consistently re-enter this state. This, in turn, supports your manifestation process. You are effectively creating a feedback loop where the passion and flow fuel your manifestation, and the results of your manifestation further fuel your passion and flow. Finding your passion through the balance of skill and challenge, and achieving a state of flow, provides a fertile ground for manifestation. This alignment offers a clear vision of your desires, enhances your focus and motivation and creates an optimal mental state for bringing your intentions to fruition.

Pragmaticism is an effective skill for managing change. One of the reasons manifesting works is that it takes a very pragmatic approach to change, encouraging individuals to examine in detail, through various means, the very specific steps that they need to take in order to attain their manifesting goal. This pragmatic approach also helps you to gain clarity about what you want to manifest. Detailed visualisation and ongoing questioning about the changes you hope to achieve helps to give you clarity about what you really want to manifest as opposed to what you think you wish to manifest. Developing pragmaticism also helps you to analyse and find solutions to the inevitable barriers that you will encounter along your manifesting journey.

Dr Darnley says, 'A lot of things can get in the way of living a life you love – insecurities, shame, comparison, perfectionism, emotions you don't know what to do with, thoughts you'd rather not have, living in a society that devalues you, etc.... I founded my private practice on the principles of "empowerment, compassion and clarity" with the intent to guide and support my clients as they uncover these traits within themselves – leading them to more balanced and fulfilling lives.' Dr Darnley is not a manifesting coach – the principles of compassion and clarity that she harnesses that are also espoused by manifesting are based on a decade of study, professional training and scientific evidence. Her methods are similar to methods frequently advocated in manifesting circles and which Amanda applies to her own personal life.

I asked Amanda to share with me an example of something that she had manifested. I was surprised when she told me that she had manifested her husband. She said, 'When I say I've manifested my husband, for some people what will come to mind is that I conjured him up out of thin air. But really, what it actually looked like was years of dating, of dating other people and then at the termination of each relationship sitting down with a list of what I liked and didn't like from the relationship and what I wanted to carry through in my next partner and what I did not. And so I ended up having quite a lengthy list of characteristics that I was looking for in a partner. And so when Casey, my husband, came along, I was very clear on what I was looking for and what I wanted. And he was it.'

Online influencer Caroline Labouchere used a vision board to manifest her house – but there is a little twist in the tail of her story. Caroline is in her fifties, a stunning, tall, slender clothes horse of a woman whose long silky grey hair is the envy of many a woman whose wiry greys are less photogenic. When I spoke to Caroline she shared her current vision board with me, displayed prominently in her bathroom. Caroline, originally from the UK, currently lives in Dubai. A few years ago she wanted to manifest a home in London and created a vision board of her perfect house. Track forward a little in time and Caroline found a house identical to the one on her vision board, the twist being that the house is not in London at all, but in Dubai. She and her husband bought the house and it has proved to be all that she imagined. Manifesting requires clarity, but also openness and an understanding that your desire may appear to you in a slightly different guise than you had initially imagined.

Gaining clarity about what you want to manifest primes your brain to draw your attention to opportunities. To avail yourself of these opportunities you must take action. The next chapter, Coherence, discusses the importance of monitoring and evaluating your own behaviour including your thoughts, beliefs and intentions to ensure that you remain on track to your goals and remain connected with and compassionate towards your true self as you bring about the change you desire.

CHAPTER FIVE

Coherence

'If one advances confidently in the direction of his dreams, and endeavours to live the life which he has imagined, he will meet with a success unexpected in common hours'

Henry David Thoreau

Alignment

Coherence, in the context of manifesting, is about ensuring that your behaviour, including your thinking, emotions and actions, is aligned and connected to your authentic self and the goals that you wish to manifest. To execute your action plan and make your vision a reality, most manifesting guides underscore the import-ance of aligning how you think, feel and act with your vision. In a nutshell, Coherence is about self-regulation, about our capacity to act to bring about Change in our long-term best interest, with Compassion, in a way that is consistent with the deepest values that we have Connected with. In a sense, manifesting is a form of self-regulation that supplements and supports the frontal lobes to exert the executive control necessary to actively pursue and create your manifesting goal.

Manifesting involves visualising and imagining your desired outcome. This process aligns with the brain's natural inclination to create predictions and build models of the world. The brain's affinity for patterns and regularities is also significant in the context of manifesting. By recognising patterns and regularities in our experiences, we can make perceptual inferences and develop expectations about how the world works. When manifesting, we can leverage this innate pattern-recognition capability to align our thoughts, beliefs and intentions with the desired outcome. By establishing a consistent mental pattern or model of our manifestation, we enhance the brain's ability to generate predictions and align our perception with the reality we want to manifest.

Understanding that the brain seeks patterns and regularities to make prediction easier can also be valuable in overcoming any limiting beliefs or doubts that may get in the way of the manifesting process. By consciously focusing on positive patterns and reinforcing the belief in the manifestation's possibility, we can enhance the brain's predictive abilities and create a stronger alignment between our internal representations and the external reality we wish to manifest.

This means we can enhance the manifesting experience by actively shaping our internal representations, aligning our thoughts and beliefs with the desired outcome. Metacognition involves monitoring and evaluating our own thoughts, beliefs and intentions, as well as assessing the quality and reliability of the information we have. This self-awareness, this connection to self, also allows us to identify any limiting beliefs, doubts or areas of uncertainty that may hinder the manifestation process.

By cultivating metacognition, we gain the ability to recognise and address any internal barriers or doubts that arise during the manifestation journey. We can examine our thought patterns, challenge negative or limiting beliefs and consciously adjust our attitudes and intentions. Metacognition empowers us to be self-reflective and proactive in managing our thoughts and emotions, creating a more supportive internal environment for manifesting.

Additionally, metacognition enables us to track uncertainty and assess the level of confidence we have in our manifestation. It helps us recognise when we may need more information, additional resources or a different approach in order to align our intentions with the desired outcome. By connecting with and staying attuned to our own uncertainties and knowledge gaps, we can make informed decisions, adjust our strategies and actively seek the necessary information or support to enhance our manifestation efforts.

Understanding uncertainty and developing metacognition are valuable elements in the practice of manifesting. They allow us to embrace the unpredictable nature of life, reflect on our own thoughts and beliefs, address any limiting factors and make informed decisions to increase the chances of successfully manifesting our desired outcomes.

In the process of manifesting, when you focus your thoughts and intentions on a specific outcome, you are essentially practising a form of inductive reasoning. Inductive reasoning involves making broad generalisations from specific observations. For example, if you observe that the sun has risen in the east every morning of your life, you might use inductive reasoning to conclude that the sun always rises in the east. It's about predicting future events based on observed patterns.

When manifesting, you may observe that when you have positive, focused thoughts and intentions you are more likely to take actions that align with those thoughts and intentions, which can then lead to achieving your desired outcomes. Over time, you might generalise this pattern to predict that focusing on positive intentions can help you achieve your goals.

Abductive reasoning, on the other hand, is often described as 'inference to the best explanation'. It involves observing a particular situation or set of data, then making an educated guess as to what caused it. For instance, if you find your garden plants wilted, you might use abductive reasoning to infer that there was a lack of rain.

Abductive reasoning might come into play when you notice a change in your life that aligns with your focused thoughts and intentions. For example, if you've been manifesting a new job opportunity, and you suddenly get a promising job offer, you might use abductive reasoning to infer that your focused intentions contributed to this outcome.

It's important to note that both inductive and abductive reasoning are prone to errors. This is primarily because both methods involve making assumptions or guesses based on available information, and those assumptions may not always be correct. Inductive reasoning can lead to overgeneralisation. This occurs when conclusions are drawn from specific instances and assumed to be true universally. For example, if you've only ever seen white swans, inductive reasoning would lead you to conclude that all swans are white. However, this conclusion would be false, because there are indeed black swans, some of which you can have the pleasure of seeing in London's Hyde Park. Overgeneralisation can also lead to biases and stereotypes.

Abductive reasoning, on the other hand, is prone to confirmation bias. This type of bias occurs when we interpret, favour and remember information in a way that confirms our existing beliefs. For instance, if you believe that a specific diet will improve your health and you start feeling better after following the diet, you might attribute your improved health to the diet (abductive reasoning) without considering other factors that might have contributed, such as increased physical activity or improved sleep habits.

Both types of reasoning are heuristics, the mental shortcuts that our brains use to simplify decision-making. While these mental shortcuts can be useful and efficient, they can also lead to errors in reasoning and judgement. This doesn't mean these reasoning methods are inherently bad or unhelpful – only that they're not fool-proof and should be used carefully, especially when making important decisions.

Of course, it's also crucial to remember that correlation does not equal causation, and many factors can influence the events in our lives. However, the practice of manifesting can potentially help guide our actions and perspective towards our desired outcomes, and inductive and abductive reasoning are part of how our brains make sense of these processes and their results.

Aligning our behaviours with our goals is a matter of self-regulation, which is a core aspect of adaptive human behaviour that allows us to make progress. Essentially, it is how manifesting works. It is something we all regularly do without consciously naming it self-regulation. For example, you might want to stay in bed when the alarm goes off, but you self-regulate and get up to go for a jog because you really want to improve your fitness and health. Basically behavioural self-regulation incorporates how you respond to situations and how your actions align with your long-term goals and core values.

Self-regulation can be broadly defined as engaging in goal-directed behaviours. A review of self-regulation co-authored by psychologist Alan Baddeley, best known for his research on working memory, says that successful self-regulation involves three main components:

1. Standards of thought, feeling or behaviour that individuals endorse, mentally represent and monitor;
2. Sufficient motivation to invest effort into reducing discrepancies between standards and actual states and;
3. Sufficient capacity to achieve this in light of obstacles and temptations along the way.

Any of us can fail to self-regulate due to a lack of standards, monitoring, motivation or capacity. Without setting standards, we can fail to achieve our health, career and relationship goals. For example: John fails on the health front because despite wanting to get fit he never sets a clear workout routine. He just vaguely thinks, 'I should exercise more.' Despite wanting to be a writer, Maria fails because she never clearly defines what kind of writer she wants to be nor does she identify what steps she needs to take to become one. Greg and Josh fail to improve their relationship because they never discuss what a 'better' relationship looks like.

Failure to monitor can also spell disaster. For example, Lisa fails to save money because she never tracks her credit-card spending and rarely checks her bank account. David fails to reduce his alcohol intake because he never takes note of how many beers he has. Mike and Sarah fail to spend more quality time together but don't actively set aside dedicated time for each other.

A lack of motivation is really limiting: giving up (guitar lessons, Pilates, art classes, training for a marathon or listening actively to your partner) because it's just too hard. Capacity or ability is also key. Emma won't excel in her job if she doesn't avail herself of the free training courses on offer at work, Carlos will never fulfil his dream of travelling the world if he never researches routes, flights, accommodation, etc. Lisa and Leo will never rebuild the trust in their relationship unless they go to couples therapy.

Self-control is a sub-set of self-regulation. Self-control is about overriding unwanted urges, disinhibiting powerful impulses and resisting temptation that might knock you off track.

Executive functions encompass a range of mental abilities, such as planning, decision-making, problem-solving, organising tasks, persistently pursuing goals, inhibiting impulsive behaviours, adapting to changing goals, resolving conflicts between goals – all things you are likely to need or encounter on your manifesting journey. Working memory is also considered an executive function. Working memory involves maintaining and manipulating information in the short term to perform complex mental manipulations like totting up the items in your shopping basket to make sure you have enough cash on you to pay for all of the items. You would also use working memory, for example, when asking for directions and remembering them until you reach your destination.

Executive processes often involve language use, judgement, abstract thinking, concept formation and logical reasoning. They are associated with specific brain networks, especially those in the frontal lobes of the brain. These processes are also referred to as central processes and are closely related to the supervisory attentional system.

Three key executive functions that are worth noting in the context of self-regulation: working-memory operations (updating), inhibition of impulses (inhibition) and mental flexibility (shifting). These functions help us remember and manipulate information, control impulsive behaviours and shift our attention between different tasks. By developing and utilising these executive functions, we can enhance our ability to regulate and thus align our thoughts, emotions and actions more successfully in pursuit of our goals. Essentially, keeping ourselves on track and focused on our manifesting objectives. Executive functions can be trained, leading to better behavioural self-regulation in the service of goals. In a sense manifesting practices and associated techniques are a form of brain training with a specific focus on the frontal lobes and executive functions.

Working memory: active representation

Working memory plays a role in mentally representing our self-regulatory goals and the strategies to achieve them. Without an active representation of goal-related information, self-regulation lacks direction and is likely to be unsuccessful unless we have established automatic self-regulatory routines or habits for managing our behaviour. It is likely that manifesting supports self-regulation by supplementing and supporting the brain's executive functions through the creation of clear goals and plans and by keeping those goals and plans to the fore through the repetition of affirmations, journaling, visualisation, vision boards and action boards. For example, visualisation exercises working memory through the repeated creation, maintenance and manipulation of detailed mental imagery.

Working memory: executive attention

Attention is a crucial part of self-regulation. Sometimes, your attention is automatically drawn to things because they are exciting or attractive, and this often competes with other things you might need or want to focus on to attain your manifesting goals. Imagine that you want to manifest a promotion at work; your action plan includes focusing on tasks that improve your job performance, like learning new skills or completing key projects. However, you might get distracted by short-term attractions, like the immediate gratification of browsing social media or engaging in office gossip during work hours. These distractions are like a tempting piece of cake when you are on a diet – they are enjoyable in the moment but do not contribute to your long-term goal of maintaining a healthy weight or earning a promotion. If you can't shift your attention away from these distractions, they take up mental space and time, leaving less energy for you to focus on your career advancement. Manifesting practices give you clarity of focus and help you to put the blinkers on and avoid distraction.

Suppose your long-term manifesting goal is achieving personal happiness, and you've determined that to attain this you need to adopt a balanced lifestyle with ample time for rest, hobbies and personal relationships. However, there might be distractions that pull your attention away from this goal. For example, you could be tempted by the immediate satisfaction of binge-watching a TV show late into the night. If you continually allow your focus to be drawn to such short-term pleasures and fail to redirect your attention to your long-term goal (having a balanced lifestyle for overall happiness), you might spend too much time on less fulfilling activities, leaving little mental space for actions that contribute to long-term happiness. These distractions, therefore, crowd out goal representation in your brain.

In both examples, your working memory capacity plays a big role in your ability to resist these attention-grabbing distractions and stay focused on your long-term goals. Developing this capacity, through manifesting techniques, could therefore help you better manage your attention, boost working memory and improve self-regulation.

Studies have shown that our working memory capacity, or how much information we can hold and process at a time, can influence how well we're able to ignore distractions. This capacity plays a big role in how well we can resist things that grab our attention. Research suggests that having a larger working memory capacity can help us proactively resist tempting things right from the start, supporting better self-regulation in the service of goal attainment.

Working memory: goal shielding

The idea of goal shielding is about focusing your attention on what you need to achieve your goal, which can help protect your goal from distractions or competing interests. Think of it like putting a protective bubble around your goal. The more you can concentrate on your goal or task, the stronger this protective bubble becomes. Goal shielding is the consequence of sustained attention to a goal or task, providing an indirect or 'passive' form of inhibitory control. In other words, this bubble is a kind of passive control method, allowing you to inhibit engaging with distractors and zoom in on what's important. In a way many of the techniques employed in manifesting act like goal shields; for example, by keeping her vision board next to her bathroom sink Caroline Labouchere stays focused on her goals. It's likely that the repeated use of goal-focused affirmations and other tools serves the same purpose.

This focused state, where you are zoomed in on your goal, is often called an action-oriented mindset in self-control research. When you're in this state, you're more focused on doing what needs to be done to achieve your goal. An important effect of successful goal shielding is that when your working memory capacity is strong, there's a closer alignment of your goal and your behaviour. Essentially, when you have a lot of mental resources available you're better able to act according to your goal. On the other hand, when your working memory capacity is low, your automatic or impulsive behaviour takes over because it's less effort and less difficult. Without a good goal shielding mechanism, you're more likely to act based on impulse rather than your goal. There's a lot of research that supports this idea. For example, one study found that people with low working memory capacity were more likely to eat sweets when tempted because they reacted based on their immediate desires. However, people with high working memory capacity were better able to resist the sweets because they were focused on their goal of not eating sweets. Manifesting works because it builds working memory capacity.

Working memory: suppression of ruminative thoughts

Ruminative thoughts are excessive, repetitive thoughts or themes that interfere with other forms of activity. Your ability to concentrate on information that's relevant to your goals can also be connected to how well you can control your own thoughts. For instance, studies have found that if you have a larger working memory capacity you're less likely to have intrusive thoughts when you're trying to suppress them. This might be because people with a larger working memory capacity are better at focusing their attention on different thoughts, which indirectly helps to suppress the thoughts they don't want to have. They are better at controlling what they think about. An interesting study showed that people with a larger working memory capacity tend to daydream less when they're doing challenging activities in their everyday life. So having a larger working memory capacity could mean you're better at keeping your thoughts on track and less likely to let your thoughts wander off task.

Down-regulation of unwanted affect and cravings

Down-regulation of unwanted affect or cravings is just a very technical way of saying reducing unwanted feelings, emotions or cravings. For instance, after a stressful day at work you might crave chocolate or a G&T when you get home. Resisting this urge by opting for a proper dinner or a calming cup of tea is an example of down-regulating cravings. During a heated argument with your boyfriend, you might feel angry. Taking deep breaths, resisting saying something nasty just to hurt or going for a walk to cool down showcases your ability to down-regulate intense emotions. Down-regulation is really important for manifesting because it allows you to manage or adjust intense emotions and desires to ensure that they better align with your manifesting goals.

Even though working memory is often thought of as a strictly thinking-related concept, it can also play a role in managing emotions. Some recent studies have shown that your working memory capacity can help you control your emotions in different ways. For example, it can help you change how you think about a situation to lessen its emotional impact (this is called cognitive reappraisal). It can also help you control how you react emotionally according to certain standards or expectations, like keeping your anger in check when you're provoked.

Recent research has solidly shown that your working memory capacity plays a big role in helping you control your actions. This applies to many things, like how you eat, how you respond emotionally and how aggressive you are. This is on top of the already well-established idea that working mental capacity helps with thinking skills and intellectual challenges. Manifesting most likely attains this through its emphasis on positive thinking.

Active inhibition of prepotent responses

Active inhibition of prepotent responses is technical jargon for our ability to actively inhibit or override behavioural responses such as habits and impulses that are not compatible with our goals. This form of inhibition is synonymous with successful self-regulation. Imagine you're at work and you receive an email from a colleague that comes off as a bit passive aggressive. Your immediate impulse might be to fire back a snarky reply or vent to a colleague. This initial reaction is a 'prepotent response', an almost automatic behaviour based on habit or in this instance emotion. Active inhibition of prepotent responses is like a mental pause button. Instead of immediately acting on your initial impulse, you take a moment to think. You remind yourself of the bigger picture – maintaining a good working relationship, keeping a professional demeanour and not escalating a minor issue. By resisting the urge to act on your initial emotional response, and choosing a more thoughtful approach, you're practising successful self-regulation. Our habits and impulses can create patterns that lead to certain memorised actions. These patterns are like pre-programmed responses that can kick into gear once they're triggered enough. Using implicit reaction time scores as a marker for impulsive predispositions, studies have shown that people who are low in behavioural inhibition are more strongly influenced by these impulsive pre-programmed responses than those high in inhibition. For example, researchers predicted who would gain weight over a year by looking at the person's impulsive food preferences and their ability to control their responses at the start of the study. Having poor control over responses has been linked to many problems related to impulse control, ranging from drug misuse and poor social responses to cheating in romantic relationships. Manifesting practices involving visualisations and affirmations can help repro-gramme our automatic responses. By regularly imagining ourselves acting in line with our goals rather than giving in to impulses, we can start to change our habitual reactions. Additionally, techniques like mindfulness meditation, often used in manifesting, can improve self-awareness and self-control, making it easier to recognise and inhibit prepotent responses.

Task-switching: shifting means versus shifting goals

Very little research has been carried out on establishing the connection between task-switching also known as mental flexi-bility or shifting. To outline a possible link between this aspect of executive function and self-regulation, Baddeley and his colleagues start with the premise that self-regulating involves solving trade-offs between the rigid pursuit of a focused goal and the possibility of being open to alternative courses of action (flexibility). Both working memory and inhibition support rigid self-regulated goal pursuit by preventing external and internal distractions. The mental flexibility of task-switching is possibly related to self-regulation in two ways; means shifting and goal shifting.

Means shifting allows us to abandon means that are sub-optimal or simply not working and pursue alternative, more effective means to reach the same goal. In contrast, goal-shifting allows us to temporarily disengage from a goal and pursue other tempting alternatives. A good example of adaptive balancing of self-regulatory goals and short-term gratification is the goal-focused dieter who allows themselves one dessert a week or one cheat day. Another way of achieving this balance would be to take a break from striving towards a goal to enjoy the successful progress made so far. It's clear from these examples that there is a fine line between adaptive balancing and self-regulation failure where the temporary break from striving becomes permanent or where the one dessert a week transforms into an everyday occurrence. This is a complex issue that hasn't fully been teased apart. A large range of situational factors can temporarily impair self-regulations, for example: alcohol intoxication, stereotype threat,[6] environmental or social stressors and depleted resources.

Scientists have pinpointed specific parts of our brain that help us handle tasks like planning and decision-making, mainly located in the frontal lobes. Two key areas in the frontal lobes help us organise our actions to reach a goal, like planning and controlling our reactions. There's a standard test that measures how good we are at these functions. When experts looked at the results, they generally found three main skills: keeping track of tasks, controlling impulses and switching between different thoughts. These three skills are crucial for everyday decision-making and organising our actions, both of which are critical for manifesting.

By supporting, improving and/or training executive functions, manifesting processes and techniques can enhance our ability to regulate and thus align our thoughts, emotions and actions more successfully.

Goal-Directed Behaviour

As we have established, manifesting requires a clear plan, the conscious creation of goals, plus ongoing action and behaviour aligned with those goals. Clinical psychologist Dr Amanda Darnley, whom we met in Chapter Four, says that manifesting is down to

---

6 an individual's expectation that negative stereotypes about his or her member group will adversely influence others' judgements of his or her performance and that a poor performance will reflect badly on the member group.

goal setting and gaining clarity around your goals. Psychologists refer to this as goal-directed behaviour, which can be divided into four stages: establishment, planning, striving, revision. When it comes to manifesting, these stages would look like: clarity about the goal you want to achieve (establishment), a plan of action (planning), implementation of the plan (striving). The fourth stage involves revising the plan in response to ongoing monitoring of progress and outcomes, allowing reflective flexibility and adaptability in response to experience and changing circumstances, contexts and desires. As we have already learned, this opportunity for revision is factored into many manifesting processes.

Having clarity about what you want and making and enacting a plan makes perfect sense and actually seems quite simple. However, what seems simple on the surface is much more challenging when you factor in how the human brain actually works. We have an amazing capacity to think rationally, to make deliberate choices and to engage in goal-directed behaviour but, and it is a big but, our behaviour is also driven by impulse. There exists a sort of tug of war between reflective behaviour and reflexive impulse. The former is effortful, conscious, far-sighted, considers the consequences of our actions and is concerned with long-term satisfaction. The latter is effortless, spontaneous, unthinking, unconcerned by broader consequences with an all-consuming concern with immediate gratification. Manifesting practices and techniques provide extra strength on the side of goal-directed reflective behaviour.

Positive psychology, a branch of psychology that focuses on the promotion of happiness and wellbeing, places significant importance on goal-directed behaviour. Positive psychology suggests that setting and pursuing meaningful goals can lead to personal growth and fulfilment. Pursuing goals can provide a sense of purpose, increase self-efficacy and foster a proactive attitude towards life. When individuals are engaged in goal-directed behaviour that is appropriately challenging and aligns with their skills, they can experience flow, which we discussed at length in Chapter Four.

Positive psychology often refers to Edwin Locke's goal-setting theory, which posits that setting specific and challenging goals leads to higher performance than setting easy or vague goals. This is because specific and challenging goals require more effort, persistence and attention. This is how manifesting works. Research in positive psychology emphasises the importance of self-concordant goals that align with an individual's intrinsic interests and values. These types of goals are more likely to be pursued over time and lead to higher wellbeing. Pursuing and achieving goals can elicit positive emotions. According to Barbara Fredrickson's broaden-and-build theory, these positive emotions can broaden individuals' thought-action repertoires, allowing them to build lasting personal resources (skills, resilience, social connections), which, in turn, can facilitate goal-directed behaviour and successful manifesting.

Neuroscience has provided several insights into the mechanisms behind goal-directed behaviour: Two areas within the prefrontal cortex play significant roles in goal-directed behaviour. They're involved in planning, decision-making and regulating behaviour based on anticipated consequences. Dopamine is crucial for motivating goal-directed behaviour. The brain releases dopamine in response to rewarding experiences, encouraging the pursuit of similar rewards in the future. The hippocampi, mentioned earlier in the context of their involvement in memory formation, also play a role in goal-directed behaviour. They help the individual recall past experiences and use this information to guide future actions. The basal ganglia, a group of subcortical structures in the brain, are involved in forming habits and routines. While not always seen as goal-directed in nature, habits can become integrated into goal-directed strategies.

Your behaviour, whether that behaviour is a habit, an innate reflex or goal-directed, is controlled by your brain. The control of goal-directed behaviour is different from that of habitual and reflexive behaviour because instead of prescribing a specific routine, procedure or action it prescribes the goal, the end-state that an action should achieve. Imagine you are trying to maintain a healthy diet (aren't we all), and your goal (G) is to lose ten pounds. You know that eating a salad (Action A) for lunch will help you move closer to this goal. Following the principle of rationality, if you're genuinely committed to losing weight you would choose the salad every time. However, in real life, it's not always so straightforward. Sometimes, even with the best intentions, you might act on impulse and opt for a cheeseburger (Action B), fries (Action C) or a milkshake (Action D) (or indeed all three) instead of a salad. Alternatively you may follow the procrastination path and perpetually push out your diet start date, promising yourself you'll start Monday.

Procrastination

The gap between what we want to do and what we end up doing can often be explained by the irrational and voluntary post-ponement of a task, despite knowing that completion of the task is the best course of action and that postponement will result in uncomfortable feelings and adverse outcomes – commonly referred to as procrastination.

Procrastination is a funny one, isn't it? Why would anyone choose to delay doing something that's in their best interest when they know that the delay will make them worse off? It's totally ir-rational. Procrastination is a perfect example of a human behaviour that illustrates the limits of rational thinking. We tend to think of our-selves as rational beings but that's not really true; it's more accurate to say that we are capable of rational thought thanks to our neo-cortex. The parts of our brains, the limbic system and the brain stem, that drive our behaviour do so in unconscious, often reflexive ways that can be irrational, particularly when future goals are pitted against immediate gratification or basic survival. We have, of course, become adept at rationalising our behaviour – I know for sure I've given perfectly rational explanations for why I've spent the day working in the garden rather than finishing the chapter I'm currently writing.

We have no way of knowing at what point in our evolution procrastination emerged but we do know that it is something that ancient Greek philosophers wrestled with. The word *akrasia*, which means weakness of will, was used by Aristotle to describe acting against one's better judgement. Socrates questioned how it could be possible that a person would do anything other than the action they deemed to be the best. It's a question that millions if not billions of us frequently ask ourselves. Why do we sabotage our own plans by doing almost anything other than what we had planned to do? Why do we continually put off until tomorrow what we can do today? Why do we leave things to the very last minute, risking missing deadlines, compromising quality and quite frankly often putting ourselves through a peculiar sort of self-inflicted torture? Despite it being the focus of examination by some of the smartest brains in philosophy, psychology, economics and other disciplines, no simple coherent answer has emerged. There are, however, some solid theories and thanks to advances in neuroscientific technology and techniques we now have some insight as to what is going on in our brains when we procrastinate.

The word itself actually stems from the Latin, 'pro' meaning forward and 'crastinatus' meaning till next day. But as the song says, 'Tomorrow Never Comes'. An interesting study that looked at Netflix viewing illustrates this beautifully. People were asked to select one movie to watch that day and one to watch at a later date. People tended to pick blockbusters or mass market comedies for their 'today' movie. In contrast, they went for serious, important, worthy films to watch at a later date. Of course, when that later date comes and they are offered the same choice, they will again succumb to the appeal of the latest blockbuster and defer the more serious choice to a later date. Whether we are talking about choosing a movie to watch later, setting aside money for retirement, fixing the gutters or writing that book the problem is that our desires shift as the long run becomes the short run. Our tendency will be to do whatever is most appealing now and push the less appealing, the challenging, our plans, the thing that we know we 'should' do into the future.

Several philosophers view procrastination in terms of conflict between 'inner selves' jostling for control. For example, the 'short-term' hedonistic self that wants a doughnut or to scroll social media (or both) battles the self that represents long-term goals like wanting to fit into a dress for the wedding next month or wanting to submit an assignment on time. Nobel prize winner Thomas Schelling argues that the self that makes plans and the self that fails to carry them out are different parts of a 'divided self' – different beings contending for control.

It's a miracle how we ever make progress towards, let alone achieve, our long-term goals. According to philosopher Don Ross we can and do attain our goals because our inner 'selves' make deals with one another. The long-term self that wants to make that essay deadline strikes a deal with the short-term self that wants to scroll social media. The bargaining key is that the short-term hedonistic self not only wants to scroll social media in the present moment but also in the future and will be open to negotiating scrolling in the future in exchange for going to the gym or researching the essay now. Procrastination on this view is a result of internal bargaining gone awry.

I am sure that you have experienced the inner dialogues, discussions, arguing and inner bargaining about what to do now and what to do in the future, as well as whether a specific choice supports or scuppers your long-term goals that these theories endeavour to explain.

From a research perspective, procrastination is mostly approached as failures of self-regulation and lack of self-control. As mentioned earlier, self-regulation is an umbrella term that encompasses reflex, non-conscious and reflexive regulatory processes, as well as what we commonly describe as 'self-control', where a person employs deliberate and conscious effort to exert control over the 'self'. Self-control, as mentioned earlier, is a specific case of self-regulation. Research suggests that self-control is a limited resource that becomes depleted with use.

Procrastination is primarily seen as an enduring personality characteristic that describes or determines a person's behaviour across a range of different situations and contexts. The personal traits of impulsivity and self-control have been repeatedly revealed by research to predict individual tendency to procrastinate. Specific characteristics of tasks make it more probable that we will procrastinate. Procrastination is likely to occur when tasks are frustrating, complicated, uncomfortable, boring, difficult, ambiguous or when they lack intrinsic reward or personal meaning. Manifesting helps people to identify goals that are personally meaningful and so should be somewhat helpful in attenuating procrastination. It's no surprise that we are likely to avoid doing tasks that we find unpleasant; this is called task aversion. 'Really dislike this task' is frequently recorded as the top reason that people procrastinate. The specific nature of tasks we find aversive will differ from one person to the next to the extent that one person's most dreaded task can be another person's favourite task. You might procrastinate over gardening, dreading cutting the grass and weeding, whereas I love gardening and it is my 'go to' procrastination activity. We are also more likely to procrastinate about tasks when the rewards associated with that task are delayed or distant in time, like writing a book. I for sure know about that one – my garden is looking really great right now.

Two accounts of procrastination hypothesise about the cognitive mechanisms that underlie it; one is about managing feelings (emotion-regulation theory) and the other is about the relationship of time to motivation (temporal motivation theory). According to the first theory, procrastination occurs when we give precedence to our current mood over our long-term goals. When we find a task aversive we rank the short-term benefits of avoiding the task higher than the long-term benefits of completing it. For example, I find a task aversive when I am unclear what is expected and when I am afraid I won't be able to deliver what I promised or what is expected. I don't like feeling unsure or fearful so I prioritise repairing my mood by doing something that makes me feel good in the present moment, like eating chocolate or pruning the hydrangeas.

Temporal motivation theory explains procrastination in terms of increasing motivation to act the closer time gets to the deadline. When the reward is in the distant future we are less motivated to engage in the task because we perceive that a task has less impact the more distant in the future it is. Our motivation to complete the task increases the closer we get to the deadline and the impact of not delivering, motivating us and increasing our willingness to act towards longer-term goals. Something I am experiencing right now as my deadline approaches.

Manifesting can be a useful tool to counter procrastination for a number of reasons. Clearly defining what you want to achieve and outlining the steps that you need to take to get there removes ambiguity and can give you a more defined path toward your goal, making you more sure of what you have to do and making it easier to start working toward it. Visualising yourself taking these steps can boost confidence and motivation, making the goal feel attainable, thereby reducing the urge to procrastinate because we fear not being up to the task. Cultivating positivity and self-belief can reduce the fear and anxiety that often lead to procrastination. Sharing your manifesting goals with friends and family can introduce an element of accountability that can make it more difficult to procrastinate. Manifesting practices can involve setting aside time for specific practices, which could help in forming habits that promote consistency and discipline, which can help us to avoid procrastination.

Habitual Behaviour

I recently watched a video on YouTube about the importance of repetition by an award-winning life coach and best-selling mani-festation author who offered advice grounded in solid science mixed with misinformation and misrepresentation of science of the kind that detracts from manifesting and leads people to refer to manifesting as pseudoscience. The manifesting author explained that repetition is key because we cultivate new habits and patterns through repetition. This is absolutely spot on and solidly supported by research and by our neuroscientific understanding of how habits are formed in the brain. However, they then state, with absolute confidence, 'it takes twenty-one days to change a habit', which is a myth that I have frequently heard perpetuated by multiple people in the self-help field. The science does not support this often-repeated claim.

Scientific research is actually relatively sparse when it comes to establishing how long it takes to form a habit. One seminal study published in 2010 indicates that it takes between 18 and 254 days to introduce a new habit. This study was carried out in the real world, in that volunteers chose a drinking, eating or activity behaviour to carry out daily for twelve weeks in the same context, for example after breakfast. The volunteers had to report their behaviour to the researchers and so it is likely that this reporting positively influenced their motivation and effort. Despite this, approximately half of the participants (ninety-six enrolled in the study, eighty-two provided sufficient data for analysis) did not perform the behaviour consistently enough to achieve the automation that confers habit status.

The volunteers had to give a daily report of how automatic the behaviour felt. Initial repetitions of their chosen behaviour led to large increases in automaticity; however, the more often they repeated the behaviour the more the increases reduced in size until automaticity plateaued. Researchers took the point at which automaticity was the highest as the point at which a habit was formed. From this the researchers calculated that it took on average sixty-six days to form a habit. This remains a best estimate of the average time it takes to form a habit rather than an absolute timeframe in which to expect a habit to form. This particular study found that participants who were working on simple habits like drinking water after breakfast peaked quicker than those trying to establish more complex habits like going for a ten-minute run before dinner. New habit formation requires effort and repetition. The amount of time it takes to automate a habit really depends on the individual, the habit itself and the context in which the desired behaviour change is occurring.

It's not absolutely clear where the pervasive twenty-one-days myth about habit formation came from, but Dr Ben Gardner, an internationally recognised expert researcher and lecturer in the psychology of habitual behaviour, surmises that it likely came from the preface of the 1960 book *Psycho-Cybernetics* where the author, plastic surgeon turned psychologist Dr Maxwell Maltz, said:

> It usually requires a minimum of about twenty-one days to effect any perceptible change in a mental image. Following plastic surgery, it takes about twenty-one days for the average patient to get used to his new face. When an arm or leg is amputated the 'phantom limb' persists for about twenty-one days. People must live in a new house for about three weeks before it begins to 'seem like home'. These, and many other commonly observed phenomena, tend to show that it requires a minimum of about twenty-one days for an old mental image to dissolve and a new one to gel.

It remains unclear how this anecdotal account from plastic surgery ended up being generalised so widely. Because it is just anecdotal, simply an observation made by Maltz, with no rigorous research to back it up.

Doctor Gardner surmises that the distinction between the term habituation and habit formation got muddled at some point. As you know, habit refers to an action that we perform repeatedly, often automatically, in a stable context, usually without conscious awareness. In contrast, when we habituate to something we get used to it; for example, with exposure we can grow accustomed to what was initially an irritating noise or an obnoxious smell. With four dogs I know that I have habituated to dog smells in my house. If I am expecting visitors, I make a point of lighting candles and I strategically place diffusers close to where I think my house guests may sit – if it's family or close friends I'll ask, 'Does my house smell of dog?' I need to ask because I can't tell any more – I no longer notice a dog smell, I have habituated to it.

It is also possible that the perpetration of the myth is related to another quote by Maltz: 'Our self-image and our habits tend to go together. Change one and you will automatically change the other.'

Dr Gardner plausibly argues that people may have erroneously assumed that because Maltz also said that it takes twenty-one days to habituate to, to get used to, a new self-image following plastic surgery that a new habit would automatically occur within the same timeframe.

How do habits work?

The internet is awash with 'habit lists' like '5 Manifesting Habits That Changed my Life' or 8 or 5 or 10 'Daily Habits to Help you Manifest your Goals'. One key reason that manifesting works is that it encourages disciples of manifesting to make goal-focused behaviour and positive thinking habitual. The repetition and the regularity of practising techniques like visualisation, affirmations and intention-setting serve to build unconscious habits that keep people on track and propel them towards their goals. Making conscious choices about habits will increase the likelihood of manifesting successfully.

To make efficient use of available energy, your brain scans your behaviour for patterns. The parts of your brain involved in conscious thinking require more energy than the activities carried out in the parts of your brain that you are not consciously aware of (see fig. 7). Our brains have an amazing energy-saving ability to carry out actions without consciously thinking about them. Habitual behaviours are an energy-efficient way for your brain to operate in the most routine circumstances. This ability to automate behaviour played a critical role in our evolution because being able to carry out routine activities without conscious effort freed up neural energy to solve problems, innovate and invent.

We need routine behaviours to prevent our brains from becoming overwhelmed by innumerable choices and decisions about how to behave and act every minute of every day. I believe there is currently an overemphasis on switching off 'autopilot'. I totally agree that it is beneficial to be present in the moment, but it is also critical for the human brain to be able to automate some behaviours. Manifesting works because the practice offers a good balance between the development of unconscious, positive, goal-oriented habitual behaviours and present-focused, goal-oriented action.

During the pandemic, many of us felt overwhelmed or experienced brain fog even if we hadn't contracted COVID. Stress and disrupted sleep did contribute to this but so too did the disruption to our routines. Pre-pandemic it was estimated that about 40 per cent of our actions each day were habits. Before COVID, with little conscious effort you followed a morning routine that involved complex actions that required your full attention when you first learned how to do them, including brushing your teeth, showering, dressing, tying shoelaces, doing up buttons, making breakfast, driving, cycling, navigating public transport or buying coffee. Over time and through repetition these complex actions were automated and became habits that you carried out with little conscious effort each morning. Likely, you rarely engaged your conscious brain until you sat at your desk to begin your first work task of the day.

When lockdown was imposed our routines were suddenly swept away. Most of us behaved randomly, we used commute times to linger in bed, and allowed Zoom meetings to dictate when, or even if, we showered or dressed. Our brains now had to make decisions about almost every aspect of our behaviour, when to get up, when to shower, when to get dressed, when to exercise or when to home school. This used up valuable resources that had previously been available to meet the demands of our jobs. The lack of structure brought about by the pandemic measures led to a strange 'holiday vibe' where we stayed up late bingeing movies, eating snacks, scrolling social media and drinking alcohol.

To conserve precious energy your brain constantly scans your behaviour for routines and patterns of behaviour that can be turned into habits. It can be any action that you perform regularly in the same place or at the same time: for example, brushing your teeth in the bathroom on waking, lighting a cigarette whenever you have a cup of coffee, criticising your own image in the bathroom mirror, reaching for the same breakfast cereal every morning, leaving for work when the 'what it says in the newspapers' comes on the radio, going to Pilates on Mondays at 8 p.m., or pouring a glass of wine while you prepare dinner.

Once your brain identifies a behaviour that you engage in routinely, such as brushing your teeth first thing on waking every morning, it transfers responsibility for that routine to a part of your brain called the basal ganglia in your limbic brain (see fig. 7). Once delegated, brushing your teeth becomes an unconscious, habitual behaviour. Your thinking brain (see fig. 7) now only has to pay attention to the initial cue at the start of the routine and check in at the end to make sure all went according to plan. Automated patterns of behaviour require little effort; this frees up energy that your brain can use for more complex activities, like solving problems, creating, innovating and other activities that will propel you towards your manifesting goals.

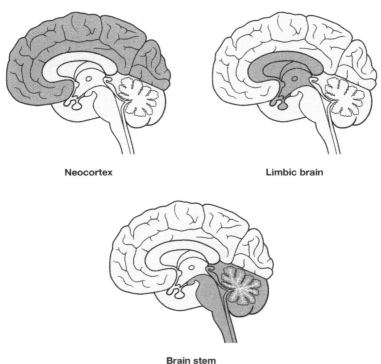

Neocortex   **Limbic brain**

Brain stem

Fig. 7: Three interconnected components of the brain: the brain stem, the limbic brain and the neocortex. The oldest part of the brain in evolutionary terms is the brain stem, which contains the brain structures that are responsible for functions that we don't have to consciously think about but which are critical to life (e.g. breathing, heart rate, blood pressure, digestion) and the cerebellum, which controls movement, balance and coordination. The limbic brain emerged in mammals about 150 million years ago to manage fight or flight circuitry, emotions, learning, memory and unconscious judgements that can strongly influence our behaviour. The neocortex, which emerged in primates 2 to 3 million years ago, is responsible for complex functions, including our ability to think, plan and use language.

Your brain doesn't make value judgements about the nature of the behaviour it automates. Its main concern in this context is to conserve energy and effort. Your brain doesn't distinguish between a healthy habit or an unhealthy one. Neither does it consider whether a particular pattern of behaviour is consistent with your manifesting goals, it just looks for patterns that can be automated in order to make the most efficient use of available neural resources.

Once a habit is formed, your thinking brain is no longer involved in making a choice or decision about that behaviour because it has relinquished control to the limbic brain. Once a habit has been established, changing it or replacing it requires energy and effort.

Cognitive control

The pursuit of manifesting goals requires behaviour change. Thankfully, the human brain is incredibly flexible and can adjust our behaviour adaptively. The considered action required to attain change and pursue specific goals requires more energy than automatic processes such as habits, heuristics and biases. Cognitive control mechanisms in the brain need to be employed to override automatic behaviours when they conflict with our goals or when they are not aligned with our planned course of action.

The prefrontal cortex plays a central role in cognitive control functions influencing our attention, our ability to inhibit our impulses, our ability to remember to do things in the future and our cognitive flexibility, which is our ability to adapt to new, changing or unexpected events. The prefrontal cortex lies directly behind the eyes and the forehead. It is the front-most portion of the neocortex (see fig. 7) and isn't fully developed until we hit our early to mid-twenties. It is the most recent part of the brain to evolve.

The prefrontal cortex plays a central role in controlling other areas of the cortex and many aspects of what we describe as our personality. It also underlies effortful processes including planning, insight and foresight that are collectively referred to as executive functions. The prefrontal cortex is incredibly well connected to other areas of the brain and is described as the executive controller.

The cognitive control required for behaviour change is more effortful and requires more energy than maintaining habits and routines. Changing your behaviour to form new habits initially requires conscious effort, but with time it becomes the new status quo, your new less effortful reality.

Interoception

When you feel hungry, thirsty, feel your heart pounding or have an urge to use the bathroom you are experiencing interoception. This just means that you are sensing internal signals from your body. Interoception is a sense just like vision, hearing, touch, taste and smell. But unlike our more familiar senses the signals received in your brain come from inside rather than outside your body. Interoception is important for recognising your emotions and your physical and mental wellbeing. A lot of research has been done on how we sense, process and perceive information from the outside world through our various senses, but less is known about how we process signals originating inside our own bodies and how these signals affect our emotional wellbeing and how we behave.

Your brain is constantly tracking internal signals from your body to make sure that all of your bodily systems are ticking over nicely and to notify you when something changes. The main purpose of interoception is to maintain balance within your body, a stable equilibrium called homeostasis. For example, your brain will notify you if you are becoming dehydrated: you will experience the sensation of thirst and be prompted to get a drink of water or a cup of tea. All interoceptive signals travel along nerve fibres and arrive at a relay station called the thalamus, a part of the brain that collects signals and passes them on to the insula – so named because it looks a bit like an island (insula is Latin for island). The insula then brings the signals into conscious awareness, making you notice that you are hungry, thirsty, feel anxious or need to pee.

For the most part, the processes involved in maintaining homeostasis are not within our conscious awareness. You are not continually, consciously, aware that your heart is beating or that you are breathing in and out all of the time. But it is possible to bring these signals into conscious awareness by paying attention.

Interoceptive accuracy refers to how good you are at feeling signals from your body. Interoceptive attention describes how often you notice the signals from your body. One individual might be more accurate at identifying body signals than others. Some individuals will pay more attention to bodily signals than others. From research we know that there are large differences between people in interoceptions. From a psychological perspective it is interesting to understand the impact that these individual interoception differences have on our behaviour, our health and our emotional wellbeing.

The other morning I entered the kitchen and noticed some blood on the floor and I said to my husband, 'Where did the blood come from, did one of the dogs cut their paw?' He said, 'I don't know, I didn't see the blood till you pointed it out.' A few seconds later I noticed that my husband's finger was bleeding and I said, 'What did you do to your hand?' When my husband looked down at his hand the realisation dawned on him that the blood on the kitchen floor was his. My husband has always been less sensitive to pain signals than I am; he frequently only notices he has cut himself when others point out the wound to him or when he looks at this injured body part by chance.

How do we know how we are feeling? How do I know whether I am happy, sad, angry, disgusted? When we experience an emotion it is usually accompanied by some bodily change such as an elevated heart rate, sweating, butterflies in your tummy or all three. Depending on the situation you might interpret the butterflies as: excitement before your team plays in the cup final; stress before you sit an exam; nervousness before making a presentation at work; or all three as you walk through the door of the coffee shop where you agreed to meet a match from an online dating app for a first date. When people experience difficulty sensing internal signals from their body they often struggle to figure out which emotion they are actually experiencing. In addition, they may also have difficulty interpreting other people's emotions. People with an anxious temperament pay extra attention to their heartbeat. As a consequence they may notice changes such as a quickening sooner than others, or they may interpret a faster heart rate as anxiety or fear while a person with a different disposition might interpret the same signal as excitement. Renaming the signal is a really useful tool for managing your emotions. For example, if one of the steps of your manifesting journey involves you doing something you have never done before, your usual pattern of behaviour might be to interpret body signals as fear, anxiety or stress – all of which can negatively affect your performance whether the task involves a job interview, going on a date or giving a talk. Renaming the feeling in your gut, the butterflies, the release of adrenaline into your gut, as excitement rather than stress can make a huge difference to you successfully achieving your manifesting goal one step at a time. People who are depressed can also have difficulty interpreting interoceptive signals with accuracy; for example, they may struggle to identify whether they feel hungry or full.

Some research suggests that interoception can help with making decisions too. This is particularly true when people are unsure about what is the right decision. For example, there is research that shows that people who are good at feeling the beat of their heart do better on a task where the aim of the game is to make money and avoid losing money. One explanation suggests that the brain remembers which sensation occurs (change in heart rate) when the individual wins money (a good outcome) or loses money (bad outcome). Over time we learn which decisions are best – even though these bodily sensations are below our conscious awareness. Individual differences in interoceptions may mean that some people rely on internal bodily symptoms to make decisions (interoceptive) while others use external information from outside the body (exteroception).

Even young children differ from each other in terms of their ability to sense their own bodies. During adolescence, a period when the brain is undergoing huge upheaval, interoception may become more difficult for some.

This chapter has explored how manifesting may help us to self-regulate, engage in goal-directed behaviour and develop goal-focused habits as well as helping us to avoid some common pitfalls that we are all vulnerable to. The next chapter focuses on understanding the psychology and neuroscience behind the most effective techniques in manifesting.

CHAPTER SIX

Create

'The best way to predict the future is to create it'
Abraham Lincoln

Manifesting Techniques

My goal for this chapter is to briefly unveil the neuroscience behind the techniques most commonly used in manifestation: affirmations, journaling, gratitude, scripting, 'faking it' (acting as if), meditation and visualisation. In this chapter we will look at what neuroscience and psychology can tell us about how each of the manifestation techniques harness the power of your brain to guide and align your thoughts, actions and experiences towards the realisation of your goals. Manifesting is about creating a new reality, a new you and indeed a new brain. Dr Tara Swart captures this notion in her book *The Source*, where she adopts a broader view of creativity that extends beyond art and ideas to the extraordinary capacity that we humans have to sculpt our own brains and our future through experience and choice.

Affirmations

Positive affirmations are statements used to challenge and overcome negative or unhelpful thoughts. Ubiquitous in manifesting,
they can be used to motivate, encourage positive life changes
and boost self-esteem, thereby replacing harmful self-talk with
more constructive narratives. They are often used as a tool in
psychology and self-help practices to encourage positive thinking
and self-empowerment, combating negative thoughts, self-
criticism and negative self-talk. Common affirmations might include
statements like 'I am capable and strong', 'I can handle whatever
comes', or 'I am deserving of success and happiness'. The idea is
that by repeating these affirmations regularly individuals can foster
a more positive self-image and attitude.

Rhonda Byrne likens affirmations to personal mission statements. Scientifically, positive affirmations are grounded in self-
affirmation theory: the idea that we are motivated to maintain
views of ourselves as a well-adapted, competent, stable and moral
individual capable of controlling important outcomes. We feel
psychological discomfort when any aspect of this self-view is
challenged. If this occurs we may attempt to alleviate the discomfort
by directly resolving the inconsistency between the self and the
new information by affirming some aspects of self in positive ways.

There are three key ideas underpinning self-affirmation theory.
The first idea is that self-affirmations help us maintain a flexible,
moral and adaptable self-narrative, contributing to our self-identity.
Unlike a rigid self-concept that sees us as fixed entities (e.g. a
'student' or a 'daughter'), self-identity allows us to adopt different
roles and identities, helping us define success in varied ways and
adapt better to different situations.

The second idea is that maintaining self-identity isn't about striving for perfection, but about being competent and adequate in areas we personally value, thereby promoting a sense of being moral, flexible and good.

The third idea is that self-integrity is maintained by behaving in ways that genuinely merit recognition and praise. Positive affirmations, then, should reflect these authentic actions and values, not just a desire for praise.

By regularly practising positive affirmations, you can rewire thought patterns to cultivate a more adaptive, positive outlook. This practice contributes to the successful manifestation of goals by nurturing motivation, self-belief and adaptability, key ingredients for any successful endeavour.

Benefits

Evidence suggests numerous benefits from daily affirmations, including enhanced self-confidence, reduced stress levels, increased physical activity, more receptivity to beneficial interventions and improved academic performance. Research has shown that self-affirmations improve problem-solving performance in underperforming, chronically stressed individuals. Some research suggests that affirmations can help reduce stress. For example, a study found that a values-affirmation intervention reduced levels of the stress hormone cortisol in individuals faced with a stressful task. They might even aid sleep quality when used in conjunction with calming practices such as meditation.

Affirmations can also promote positive health behaviour change that is difficult to achieve through public health advice. For example, a series of studies showed that self-affirmation can increase individuals' openness to health-risk information and promote health behaviour change. Some research suggests that affirmations can boost academic performance. For instance, one study found that a self-affirmation exercise improved grade-point averages of minority middle-school students over two years.

Affirmations allow us to engage with self-improvement initiatives more openly. Furthermore, affirmations, particularly healing affirmations, can foster an optimistic attitude, promoting resilience and aiding in both physical and emotional healing. Affirmations can also transform our outlook on life. By helping us construct more hopeful narratives about ourselves, affirmations can significantly reduce our tendency to dwell on negative experiences. To boost self-esteem, affirmations should reflect core personal values and focus on reinforcing your sense of self-identity.

While the words 'affirmations' and 'mantras' are often used interchangeably, they differ slightly: mantras typically carry spiritual significance, while affirmations are designed to encourage positive feelings, thoughts and attitudes, with no religious connotation.

The impact of affirmations can vary based on many factors, including the personal relevance and repetition of the affirmations the individual's initial attitude and the context in which they're used. While not a panacea for all challenges, when used appropriately affirmations can serve as one of many tools for promoting positive psychological change and wellbeing.

However, it is important to remember that affirmations are not magical cures for mental health issues such as anxiety or depression. While they can supplement clinical treatment by promoting adaptive cognitive processes, they should never replace professional help.

Neuroscience

There is some neuroscientific evidence that supports the efficacy of affirmations. While this area of study is still developing and more research is needed for definitive conclusions, the preliminary findings are promising: the practice of positive affirmations can be linked to neuroplasticity, the brain's ability to adapt and change with learning throughout a person's life. Repeatedly thinking positive thoughts or affirmations can help to strengthen the associated neural pathways. This principle is often summed up as 'neurons that fire together, wire together', meaning the more you engage in a particular pattern of thinking, feeling or behaving, the stronger the neural connections in that network become.

Neuroscientific research shows that practising daily affirmations activates the part of the brain involved in positive valuation and self-related information processing. This suggests that positive affirmations not only help us view self-relevant information more positively, but they also change our brain's pathways.

Positive affirmations can affect our self-perception and self-worth, which are associated with activity in the Default Mode Network of the brain. You may recall that this network is involved in self-referential processing – in other words, thinking about yourself. It's suggested that practising affirmations could strengthen positive associations in this network.

Using positive affirmations may reduce activity in the brain's fear centre, the amygdala, which is integral to the stress response. As a consequence, affirmations may help create a more balanced brain response to stress or perceived threats. One study used fMRI to demonstrate that self-affirmation leads to neural changes in areas associated with 'positive valuation' and 'self-related processing'. While not directly linked to affirmations, it's known that positive thinking and a positive mood can boost production of serotonin, a neurotransmitter that contributes to feelings of wellbeing and happiness. It's plausible, therefore, to suggest that positive affirmations could potentially contribute to increased serotonin levels.

In sum, while research is still evolving, there is neuroscientific evidence suggesting that affirmations can influence brain activity and potentially lead to positive psychological outcomes. As with many psychological techniques, individual results can vary, and what works well for one person might not work as well for another. In fact, the effectiveness of affirmations can vary widely from person to person, and, while they can be a powerful tool for change, the best advice would be for them to be used as part of a broader strategy for improving self-compassion, self-love and self-worth. According to this theory, we maintain our sense of self-integrity, or our perceived ability to control outcomes and respond flexibly to threats to our self-concept, by affirming our beliefs in positive ways.

Faking It

'Fake it till you make it' and 'act as if' are synonymous and popular phrases in self-help literature. Fake it till you make it is something I advise in the context of smiling.

Let me explain. When you smile, your brain gets a feel-good kick, releasing chemicals like dopamine, serotonin and endorphins. These chemicals contribute to feelings of happiness, work as natural antidepressants and can even relieve pain. This means that the simple act of smiling not only expresses happiness, but it also helps create it. Another cool thing your brain does when you smile is release little molecules called neuropeptides. These help to dial down your stress and beef up your ability to bounce back from tough situations. Surprisingly, smiling doesn't need to be a result of feeling happy – it can also be the cause of it. You might think of a smile as something that just happens when you're feeling good, but even a fake smile can trick your brain into releasing these happiness-inducing chemicals. By just choosing to smile, you can actually improve your mood and brain health.

Additionally, humans have a natural tendency to copy the actions of others due to the mirror neurons in our brains. These neurons respond both when we perform an action and when we see someone else perform it. When you see someone else smile, your brain responds by not only making you smile too but also by creating genuine feelings of happiness. This means that seeing a smile doesn't just make you respond with a surface-level, synthetic smile, it can also spark real joy within you.

In the context of manifesting, faking it till you make it and acting as if require you to behave in ways that align with your desired outcome, even before it's achieved. For example: consider a situation where you want to become a morning person. Even if you're not, you might start acting as if you already are one. Set your alarm early, resist the snooze button and get out of bed immediately. Plan morning activities that excite you, such as a delightful breakfast or a refreshing walk. Gradually, your brain will adapt to this new routine. You might find yourself waking up early without the alarm and enjoying the extra hours of the day. The idea is that, by acting as if you are a morning person, you start to believe you are, you start to behave as if you are and, over time, you become a morning person.

Benefits

The principle underlying 'act as if' and 'fake it till you make it' aligns with several psychological theories and research findings.

One relevant theory is the self-perception theory proposed by psychologist Daryl Bem. According to this theory, people some-times infer their inner states – such as attitudes, beliefs and emotions – from their own behaviour. So, if you're acting confidently (even if you initially don't feel confident), you might observe your behaviour and infer that you are indeed a confident person. Over time, this may lead to genuine feelings of confidence.

The concept of embodied cognition also supports this principle. Embodied cognition refers to the two-way interaction between our bodies and brains: our brain influences our bodily actions, and in return our bodily actions can influence our mental states. A well-known study found that adopting 'power poses' (body postures associated with confidence and success) can lead to hormonal and behavioural changes that correspond with greater confidence and stress resilience.

Neuroscience

In terms of neuroscience, our behaviours and experiences can shape our brains through neuroplasticity. This suggests that practising new behaviours can lead to changes in brain pathways that support those behaviours. For instance, research has shown that cognitive behavioural therapy (CBT), which often involves 'acting as if' by trying out new behaviours, can lead to observable changes in brain circuitry.

That said, while these theories and findings suggest that faking it till you make it can be a valuable strategy, it's important to approach this practice with authenticity and self-awareness. Acting as if you're a confident public speaker can help you become one, but pretending to have skills or qualifications that you don't possess can lead to stress, ethical issues and potential failures. The goal is to use this strategy as a tool for growth and self-improvement, not as a mask for deception or self-delusion. Faking it till you make it can reshape our behaviours and attitudes. It doesn't mean being untruthful to yourself or others. Instead, it's about stepping out of your comfort zone and adjusting your thinking, attitudes, behaviours and habits to bring positive change in your life.

More research is needed to fully understand the neural mechanisms underlying faking it till you make it and to identify the most effective ways to apply this strategy.

Gratitude

Gratitude, a powerful human emotion, is a 'state of thankfulness' or 'being grateful', often tied to receiving benefits from others. It's seen as a positive emotional response that helps in acknowledging the good things in life. Practising gratitude helps us appreciate the good things already in our lives, shifting us away from our tendency to focus more on the negatives and life's obstacles. Gratitude serves as a motivating force propelling us forward. Regular practice of gratitude can transform our brain's functionality, enhancing psychological wellbeing and thereby increasing the likelihood of achieving personal and professional manifesting goals. Dr Darnley advocates using a gratitude journal because she feels that an important part of manifesting is to remain grateful for each step that takes you closer to your goal. She believes that keeping a gratitude journal keeps you in a positive space, preventing you from beating yourself up because you haven't reached your goal yet.

Importantly, gratitude is associated with many of the things in life that people wish to manifest, most notably happiness. People who practise gratitude derive more happiness and pleasure from everyday life. One effective gratitude exercise involves writing detailed, heartfelt notes to individuals who have positively influenced your life. This practice elicits feelings of contentment and takes surprisingly little time. Another popular strategy is keeping a gratitude journal, where you record all things, big and small, for which you are thankful. This focus on positive memories can also help resurrect past joyful experiences. Although the effects of gratitude are not instant, once initiated they persistently impact our physical and psychological health. This power of gratitude echoes the saying 'it is not happiness that brings us gratitude. It is gratitude that brings us happiness.'

Benefits

Gratitude has been found to carry substantial psychological benefits, including increased self-satisfaction, improved mood, enhanced alertness and more positive emotions and thoughts. These benefits, in turn, contribute to better communication, greater empathy, stronger interpersonal relationships and more active team participation. Gratitude also bolsters happiness by inducing positive emotions, primarily contentment and pleasure. Simple practices, such as keeping a gratitude journal, complimenting yourself or sending thank you notes, can instantly lift your mood. For couples, expressing gratitude to each other fosters mutual trust and loyalty, leading to lasting, happier relationships. Gratitude awakens you to the beauty of life and the world.

Furthermore, gratitude is tied to increased vitality, energy and enthusiasm to work harder, which is beneficial in terms of proactive manifestation. Gratitude not only enhances personal wellbeing but also bolsters professional commitment. Managers who express gratitude cultivate a more cohesive, productive team environment, fostering compassion, empathy and positive group dynamics. Workers who express gratitude are generally more productive and responsible, fostering closer interpersonal bonds. This practice leads to increased volunteering for assignments and stronger team participation.

On the health front, research suggests a strong link between gratitude and good health, both mental and physical. Activities like keeping a gratitude journal can lower stress levels, improve sleep quality and enhance emotional awareness. Gratitude can also help alleviate pain. Research revealed that patients who kept a gratitude journal reported less pain and were more cooperative with treatment. One way gratitude improves physical health is by regulating metabolic functions and hormonal imbalances. Gratitude practices can even reduce symptoms of several conditions like cardiac diseases, inflammation and neurodegeneration.

Stress, both positive (eustress) and negative (distress), is a natural response to change and so, given that manifesting fundamentally involves bringing about change, managing stress is crucial to successful manifesting. Gratitude has been found to be a natural stress detox, effectively releasing stress hormones and fostering positive emotions. Practising gratitude can help us manage stress more effectively, appreciate life's little joys and navigate present circumstances with heightened awareness and perception. Gratitude has a profound impact on mental health. Regularly expressing gratitude can help mitigate stress, and its effects permeate all aspects of wellbeing – physical, mental and social.

Research by mental health specialist Robert Emmons reveals that a regular gratitude practice reduces various negative emotions. Due to its effectiveness in anxiety reduction, gratitude practices like journaling and group discussions have become integral components of mental health interventions and life coaching, delivered by psychologists and other health professionals. Such practices have shown particular efficacy in treating PTSD, social phobia, death phobia and nihilism. In essence, fostering an attitude of gratitude not only rewires our brain for positivity but also equips us with the psychological strength needed to achieve our life goals.

Anxiety, which often leads to feelings of insecurity and the questioning of personal strengths, can be mitigated through gratitude. The book *Grateful Brain* by Alex Korb suggests that consciously practising gratitude can retrain our brain to prioritise positive emotions and thoughts, reducing anxiety and apprehension. Recent research substantiates these ideas, with a study showing that gratitude exercises decreased death anxiety in older adults. Gratitude seems to help us accept life's uncertainties and feel less fearful about the future.

Even in dealing with depression, gratitude proves beneficial. It facilitates a shift in focus from burdens to the blessings around us. Particularly, gratitude exercises can expedite recovery from depressive episodes, fostering a stronger motivation to overcome distress. Practising gratitude daily can potentially have effects akin to antidepressants, providing a sense of long-lasting happiness and contentment. Over time, this regular practice strengthens these neural pathways, helping cultivate a lasting, inherently positive and grateful nature. Hence, gratitude can be an influential tool in achieving personal and professional goals, as it strengthens psychological wellbeing, enhances social bonds and promotes brain changes conducive to happiness and productivity.

Gratitude can cultivate resilience, allowing individuals to adapt and cope more effectively with life's challenges. It enhances positive emotions like happiness, satisfaction and pleasure, equipping us with the emotional strength to manage stress. Research has also shown a strong correlation between gratitude and resilience, with grateful individuals displaying increased happiness and emotional strength.

People who regularly express gratitude, whether through a journal or verbally, tend to be more empathetic and positive. Emotional resilience consists of several components, including social competence, problem-solving, autonomy, forgiveness and empathy. Current studies suggest that gratitude could be a sixth component. It promotes positivity, combats negative thinking, keeps us grounded in reality, focuses on solutions and strengthens interpersonal relationships. Overall, by instilling an attitude of gratitude, we can develop resilience and mental strength, equipping ourselves with the tools needed to pursue and achieve our life goals.

Neuroscience

Neurologically, gratitude can create changes in the brain that lead to the many benefits listed above. By practising gratitude, we can potentially increase our likelihood of achieving manifesting and other life goals, due to its effects on enhancing our psychological wellbeing, social relationships and overall health. Gratitude, therefore, offers a simple but powerful means to foster personal growth and happiness.

Neuroscientific research reveals fascinating insights about the effects of gratitude on the brain. Ancient cultures revered gratitude, but only recently have scientists started exploring its neural basis. Expressing and feeling gratitude correlates with a higher volume of grey matter in a brain area linked with moral judgements involving feelings of gratefulness. Moreover, gratitude 'wires and fires' neural connections to the brain's bliss centre, promoting cognitive restructuring through positive thinking and reducing fear and anxiety by regulating stress hormones.

Crucially, regular expressions of gratitude stimulate the release of dopamine and serotonin, neurotransmitters tied to feelings of pleasure, reward, motivation, satisfaction, happiness and optimism. This stimulation makes us feel good, boosting our mood instantly and motivating us to repeat the behaviour. Additionally, it boosts the production of noradrenaline, which regulates the stress responses. Individuals expressing gratitude show reduced levels of the stress hormone cortisol, resulting in better cardiac functioning and increased resilience to emotional setbacks.

Gratitude has a transformative impact on our brains and overall wellbeing. According to UCLA's Mindful Awareness Research Center, practising gratitude alters the neural structures in our brain, making us happier and more content. Gratitude stimulates the release of feel-good hormones and promotes efficient immune system function.

This seemingly simple gesture of expressing gratitude profoundly influences our brain and biological functioning. Importantly, the effect on the brain is enduring, reducing not only stress, anxiety and depression but also bodily pain. Gratitude plays a key role in releasing toxic emotions by activating the hippocampus and amygdala, the brain areas responsible for emotions and memory. Studies found that writing gratitude letters significantly enhanced mental health recovery compared to journaling negative experiences. The reduction in pain reported by patients keeping a gratitude journal is likely due to gratitude's role in regulating dopamine levels, promoting vitality and reducing subjective feelings of pain.

Improvement in quality of sleep likely occurs because the expression of gratitude activates the hypothalamus, a part of the brain involved in regulating numerous bodily functions, including sleep. A brain imbued with gratitude and kindness is more likely to achieve deep, restful sleep and wake up refreshed and ready to work on manifesting goals.

Gratitude exercises have been found to stimulate neuro-transmitters responsible for positive emotions, helping counteract depression's demotivating effects. Gratitude also increases the neural modulation of a brain region involved in managing negative emotions. On a neurobiological level, gratitude regulates the sympathetic nervous system, which triggers anxiety responses. Psychologically, it trains the brain to discard negative ruminations and concentrate on positive thoughts.

Gratitude's activation of the brain's reward centre changes how we perceive ourselves and the world around us. By focusing on the positive aspects of life, gratitude encourages our brain to appreciate what we have, thereby cultivating intrinsic motivation and present-moment awareness.

The neuroscience of gratitude is a rapidly developing field, and more research is needed to fully understand the brain mechanisms involved.

Journaling

Journaling, in a psychological or therapeutic context, is the act of writing down your thoughts, feelings, experiences, goals or ideas, typically in a structured and consistent way. It can serve multiple purposes, such as providing a way to express emotions, tracking progress towards goals, fostering self-awareness or simply serving as a memory aid.

Benefits

As for the scientific evidence supporting its efficacy, there is substantial research that suggests journaling can have several benefits: expressive writing, where individuals write about traumatic, stressful or emotional events, has been found to lead to improved mood, greater psychological wellbeing and reduced stress levels. This may be due to the therapeutic effect of expressing and structuring thoughts and feelings in writing. Journaling can improve cognitive functioning, as it promotes the integration of complex ideas and facilitates problem-solving.

Writing about stressful or traumatic events can help individuals process the events and reduce some of the negative effects associated with these experiences. Of particular relevance to manifesting is the finding that journaling about goals can boost motivation and commitment, making individuals more likely to achieve their goals. It can also provide insights into patterns of behaviour, which can be useful for behaviour-change interventions. Some research has found that expressive writing can also have physical health benefits, including improved immune system function, decreased blood pressure, improved lung and liver function and improved sleep.

Journaling can be a beneficial intervention for those with mental health disorders like depression, anxiety or post-traumatic stress disorder (PTSD). It can provide a safe outlet for emotions and help individuals better understand and manage their symptoms. While the benefits can vary from person to person and depend on how journaling is used, overall the evidence suggests that it can be an effective tool for enhancing psychological wellbeing and promoting personal growth.

Neuroscience

There is neuroscience research suggesting that the practice of journaling can have a significant impact on the brain, leading to numerous mental and emotional health benefits.

Emotional Processing: the act of writing about your thoughts and feelings has been found to activate the brain's ventrolateral prefrontal cortex, an area involved in thinking about yourself and about your emotions. This can help you to better process and understand your emotions, which, in turn, can lead to improved emotional wellbeing.

Reduced Stress: journaling about stressful events can help you to manage and reduce stress by enhancing the function of the amygdala, the brain's fear centre. This can help you to more effectively manage your emotional responses to stress, which can result in decreased feelings of anxiety and distress.

Improved Memory: when you journal, you are using both the parts of your brain that deal with language and words and the parts of your brain that deal with visual and sensory information. This dual activation can help to improve memory and recall.

Trauma Healing: writing about traumatic events can facilitate the brain's processing of the event, allowing for healing and reduction of post-traumatic stress disorder symptoms. This is believed to be due to the way writing influences the brain's hippocampus, which plays a key role in encoding traumatic memories.

Cognitive Functioning: regular writing and articulation of thoughts can stimulate the parts of the brain responsible for cognition and learning, thus improving cognitive function over time.

While journaling can be an effective tool for mental and emotional health, it is not a substitute for professional help when dealing with serious mental health issues.

Meditation

Meditation is a practice that has been used for thousands of years. It involves techniques such as mindfulness and focus, the purpose of which is to train attention and awareness, which having read this book you know are key reasons that manifesting works. People who regularly engage in practices associated with manifesting, religion and spirituality, including meditation, affirmations, contemplation, prayer or deep reflective thought, have enhanced attentional abilities. This section on meditation will outline the general benefits of meditation and the neurological underpinnings.

Benefits

Meditation has been associated with a variety of positive outcomes. One of the most well-known benefits of meditation is reduced levels of stress. Regular meditation practice can lead to improvements in attention span and focus. Executive functions such as working memory capacity can be improved through mindfulness meditation. Meditation has been found to lead to improvements in self-image and a more positive outlook on life. Regular meditation can also help reduce insomnia and improve sleep quality. Numerous studies have shown the efficacy of meditation. For instance, a meta-analysis published in *JAMA Internal Medicine* found that meditation helps reduce anxiety, depression and pain. Another study found that long-term meditators have altered resting brainwave patterns, suggesting they have a different subjective experience even when not meditating. Research shows that meditation can slow down the ageing process and lead to physical benefits as well, such as reduced blood pressure. Many of these benefits can be experienced by quieting your inner voice for a mere ten to fifteen minutes a day.

Of course, meditation isn't a cure-all, and its effectiveness can depend on the consistency of practice and the individual's unique needs and circumstances. But it can certainly serve as a valuable tool for promoting mental and physical wellbeing.

Neuroscience

From a neuroscience perspective, meditation can have several impacts on the brain. Long-term meditation can lead to changes in brain structures. For instance, research using MRI scans has shown increased grey matter density in the prefrontal cortex (associated with decision making and self-control), the hippocampi (associated with learning and memory) and other areas related to emotional regulation in people who regularly meditate. All of these changes would benefit brain health and also improve brain function.

When neuroscientists measured brain activity in Buddhist monks while they meditated, they found that the monks who had been practising meditation for a long time had more organised and stronger attentional brain systems than study participants who were just learning to meditate. Meditation and possibly other contemplative practices change how the brain is wired, dialling up attention and dialling down areas of the brain that focus on the self.

The Default Mode Network, the network of brain regions that's active when the brain is at rest and not focused on the outside world, tends to be less active in experienced meditators. This suggests that meditation may help to improve focus and attention. During meditation the slower alpha and theta waves, associated with relaxed wakefulness, are more prevalent. Meditating regularly can also reduce activity in the amygdala, leading to lower stress levels. Regular meditation practice can increase neuroplasticity. This increased neuroplasticity can help improve memory and learning capabilities and enhance emotional regulation, all of which can increase the likelihood of successful manifesting.

Positive Thinking

Positive thinking, from a psychological standpoint, refers to an optimistic attitude that focuses on the bright side of life and antici- pates positive outcomes. It's often associated with concepts like positive affirmations, optimism and positive visualisation. This does not mean ignoring the negative aspects of life, but rather approaching them in a more productive and positive way. While positive thinking is beneficial, it doesn't mean that you should ignore or suppress negative emotions. It's crucial to acknowledge and process negative feelings as well. The aim is to develop balanced and realistic thinking and avoid tipping into 'toxic positivity', which is the overgeneralisation of a happy or optimistic outlook, to the point where it minimises or invalidates genuine emotional pain or complexity. It is positivity pushed to an extreme, where any negative emotions are seen as undesirable or taboo. Rather than offering a balanced perspective that allows space for the full range of human emotions, toxic positivity involves maintaining a positive facade at all costs. To do so can be detrimental on multiple levels. Emotionally, it stifles the natural process of coping with difficulties. Psychologically, it can enforce a kind of emotional stoicism that prevents people from fully processing their experiences. In relation- ships, it can create distance and misunderstandings, as one person may feel their emotions are being dismissed or trivialised. Essentially, toxic positivity offers a narrow, unhelpful narrative that reinforces the idea that 'good vibes only' are acceptable, thereby undermining the complex tapestry of human emotional experience.

Benefits

Positive emotions and thoughts have been linked to lower stress levels, better immune-system function and overall better health. A positive outlook can also contribute to longevity and has been linked with a variety of health benefits, including lower rates of depression, better cardiovascular health and greater resistance to common colds.

Neuroscience

Neuroscience has provided some evidence to suggest that positive thinking can have real, measurable effects on the brain and body. Neuroplasticity, the brain's ability to reorganise itself by forming new neural connections throughout life, can be influenced by positive thinking, as repeated positive thoughts can strengthen these neural connections over time. Positive thoughts and emotions can influence brain activity, particularly in areas like the prefrontal cortex (associated with decision-making and social interactions) and the amygdala (associated with emotions).

Scripting

Scripting is a tool used in the practice of manifestation. It involves writing down your desires or goals as if they have already happened, often in great detail. The idea is to fully immerse yourself in the feelings and attitude of having already achieved your goals, thereby aligning yourself with the desired outcome and helping to make it a reality. This technique is closely tied to concepts such as positive visualisation and affirmations.

Benefits

The scientific support for scripting, specifically, is limited. However, there is evidence from neuroscience and psychology to support some of the general principles behind scripting. Self-fulfilling prophecy is a well-documented psychological phenomenon whereby believing something can make it more likely to happen. If you believe you'll succeed and thus act in ways that further your goals, you're more likely to actually achieve those goals. There's a wealth of research showing that mental imagery, aka visualisation, can impact cognition, emotion and behaviour. By visualising your desired outcomes, you may be able to enhance motivation, increase self-confidence and improve performance.

Neuroscience

The brain is constantly changing in response to our thoughts, behaviours and experiences. Positive, goal-directed thoughts and emotions can strengthen certain neural pathways and potentially influence our behaviour and reality over time.

In sum, there is little research on scripting directly but rather the broader principles of visualisation, self-fulfilling prophecy and self-directed neuroplasticity. Also, it's important to balance positive thinking and goal setting with a realistic assessment of obstacles and challenges.

Vision Boards

Vision boards are a tool often used in manifestation. They are typically collages of images, words and phrases that represent the person's dreams, goals, aspirations and desired outcomes. The idea is that, by visually representing your dreams and desires, you can more effectively focus your thoughts and emotions on them, which may increase your chances of achieving them. It is usual to place the vision board somewhere prominent as a constant reminder of your goals. Dr Darnley says that she personally uses vision boards because she is a visual person who likes having things that she can look at quickly to set an intention. In fact, vision boards are something that she uses regularly with her clients: 'When we're talking about goals, and we talk about building a life worth living, or a life worth loving, I like to say, what does that life look like?'

Benefits

From a psychological perspective, vision boards can serve a few important functions. Creating a vision board requires you to clarify your goals and ambitions. This can make your dreams seem more concrete and achievable, and help you determine the steps you need to take to achieve them. Having a visual representation of your goals can help you keep them at the forefront of your thoughts. This can improve your focus and motivation, making you more likely to take the necessary steps towards your goals. By visualising your desired outcomes, you can cultivate positive emotions and beliefs associated with achieving them. This can improve your motivation and self-belief, and may even influence your subconscious mind.

Neuroscience

While there is no specific neuroscientific research on the use of vision boards, it is not unreasonable to speculate that they might work in a number of ways. By regularly viewing your vision board, you repeatedly expose yourself to stimuli related to your goals. This can prime your brain to notice opportunities and take actions that align with these goals. The reticular activating system (RAS) is a network in the brain that plays a key role in focus and attention. By focusing on the images and words on your vision board, you could potentially engage the RAS, helping you to spot opportunities that align with your goals.

While vision boards can be a helpful tool for goal setting and motivation, achieving your goals also requires taking appropriate actions, and some goals may require skills, resources or opportunities that aren't within your control. There is limited empirical research specifically on the efficacy of vision boards. However, the broader psychological and neuroscience concepts that they draw upon (goal setting, visualisation, priming) are well-supported in the literature.

Visualisation

Visualisation, which I have mentioned several times throughout the book, is probably the most talked-about manifesting technique. You'd be forgiven for thinking of it exclusively as a manifesting technique, possibly even one that needs to be taught or learned, but the fact of the matter is that we do it without thinking every day. You have probably been visualising your entire life. For hundreds of thousands of years humans have harnessed the ability to visualise and manifest a yet-to-exist future. Our ancestors visualised and manifested shelters from the elements, strategic hunting groups and tools that would revolutionise their world. Visualisation is the ace up our species' sleeve.

Creating a dream life, manifesting a desired future, depends on our capacity to look forward and plan for a potentially controllable future. The ability to imagine the future bestowed on us an incredible evolutionary advantage. Being able to plan for the future, the ability to think beyond our immediate needs in the now, makes survival more likely.

Visualisation is influenced by past experience and memories. To visualise the future in the now, you need to access the past. It is your past experiences, your memories, that influence how you imagine the future. When you visualise meeting your friend for lunch at your favourite restaurant tomorrow you instinctively use your recollections of past visits there with your friend. In addition to 'seeing' the interior of the venue, the décor, the seating configuration, your visualisation will possibly evoke several sense memories such as the smell of garlic, the sound of the maître d's accent, the taste of the fig chutney, the heat of sun through the window at your favourite table. Your visualisation may have emotional salience as you recall the fun that you and your friend have had in this restaurant.

When you imagine something you have never experienced before – let's say attending a book launch for the first time – your brain will piece together information, taking relevant bits and pieces from your memories and life experiences to create a mental simulation, a visualisation, of what the book launch might be like. A sort of best-guess mental representation. You may have been in the specific book shop before but never at a book launch, so you might set the scene in some familiar space in the store, you may have the author at a desk signing books, surrounded by posters and lots of people drinking wine holding copies of the book in their hands. These images may come from images you've seen of book launches on social media, in magazines or in movies.

The incredible power of visualisation is best demonstrated in patients who have experienced paralysis in a limb following a stroke. When a person experiences a stroke as a consequence of a blocked brain artery, the brain tissue fed by that artery dies because it is deprived of the blood that provides it with the oxygen and nutrients essential for survival. Tissue death then spreads to the surrounding areas, causing more damage. When stroke patients visualise moving the affected arm or leg, blood flow to the affected area of the brain increases, saving the surrounding brain tissue and limiting the amount of damage caused by the stroke.

Visualisation has been harnessed by athletes, musicians and actors to enhance performance or learn skills. Detail is key. And this is something that the manifesting community have picked up on. A picture paints a thousand words. When you create a detailed visual image, your brain will pay attention and respond as if it is actually carrying out the actions that you are visualising. Scientific studies show that detailed visualisation has allowed athletes to attain goal times, improved bar clearance in high-jumpers and enabled gymnasts to execute complex tricks for the first time.

Psychologists have long recognised the benefits of visualisation in behavioural therapy.

Visualisation or mental imagery involves the sense of having 'pictures' inside your head. Such images may be memories of earlier visual experiences or syntheses produced by the imagination (e.g. visualising a pink lemon). Visual imagery can be used for such purposes as dealing with traumatic events, in desensitisation work or improving physical performance. Visualisation can also contribute to anxiety and many mental health issues if we habitually visualise negative outcomes or worst-case scenarios.

One thing that is rarely, if ever, mentioned is the fact that the ability to visualise varies significantly across individuals. At one end of the spectrum, you have individuals with hyperphantasia, an exceptionally vivid visual imagination. These people can conjure up intricate scenes, down to the minutest details, as if they are experiencing them in real life.

On the opposite end are those with aphantasia, a condition characterised by an inability to create mental images. People with aphantasia may understand concepts and remember facts but can't visualise them. Reading a descriptive passage in a book doesn't conjure up images but rather a conceptual understanding of the narrative.

Between these two extremes lies a continuum of visual imagination, with most people falling somewhere in the middle. Some can visualise clearly but not control the images well, while others may be able to manipulate fuzzier mental images with ease. Several factors contribute to these individual differences, ranging from neurological structure and function to past experiences and learned strategies. Individual differences in visualisation ability may affect how people learn, plan and problem-solve, which could make the process of manifesting more challenging for some.

Benefits

Visualisation, also known as mental imagery or mental rehearsal, has been scientifically studied in a variety of fields, revealing numerous benefits. Athletes who incorporate visualisation into their training often see improvements in their performance. This includes better accuracy, increased confidence and a stronger mental state. By imagining themselves practising or competing, they can reinforce the physical skills they need without actual physical exertion. Research has shown this can enhance muscle memory and improve subsequent performance.

Visualisation can be used as a relaxation technique, where individuals imagine themselves in calming or pleasant situations.

This can lead to reduced stress and anxiety levels.

Visualisation can also help to build confidence and motivation. For instance, envisioning successful completion of a task can boost self-confidence and make the task seem more achievable, which is of key relevance in terms of how manifesting works. Medical trainees have used visualisation to mentally rehearse surgical procedures before performing them, which has been found to improve their performance. Visualisation has been used in pain management, where patients imagine a more positive scenario or divert their focus away from the pain.

Neuroscience

As for the neuroscience of visualisation, it is thought to work by forming new neural pathways and strengthening existing ones in the brain, similar to how physical practice does. When we visualise, we engage many of the same brain regions as when we actually perform the action. This can reinforce the neural connections involved in the action, making it easier to perform in the future. Regularly visualising achieving your goals could potentially prime your brain for success.

So there you have it; these key manifesting techniques are beneficial in numerous ways that not only help us to attain our manifesting goals but also improve our mental wellbeing, our sense of contentment and happiness as well as our quality of life.

Conclusion

If you take one thing away from this book, let it be that the power to manifest lies within you, within your brain. What happens inside your brain is the most magnificent magic show on earth. Manifesting is not supernatural, it's natural. Manifesting is not magic, it's science. With this book I hope to have given you a better understanding of that science. Manifesting works because it harnesses the power of your amazing brain through Compassion, Connection, Change, Clarity and Coherence and uses techniques backed by science to Create the reality you desire.

COMPASSION

Compassion for yourself is foundational for successful manifesting. Swapping self-criticism for self-kindness is key. No matter what our individual manifesting goals look like, at the end of the day we all seek happiness and contentment, which are among the many benefits of self-compassion.

Manifesting techniques such as affirmations, meditation and positive thinking help us to be kinder to ourselves and activate areas of the brain related to positive emotions and positive self-talk.

Self-compassion is a powerful way to trigger the release of the hormone oxytocin, boosting self-confidence, optimism, social interaction and your health.

Core Concept: be kind to yourself and commit to a loving and supportive relationship with yourself till death do you part. Stay balanced and avoid focusing too much on any one thing. Share the ups and downs of life, nurture connection with others.

CONNECTION

Connecting with your true self is critical to successful manifesting. If you want to change your life you must first know yourself. Your brain constructed your sense of self using information that could well be obsolete or untrue. Manifesting promotes self-awareness, encouraging you to question limiting beliefs and the origins and veracity of the story of you that is embedded in the neural circuitry of your brain.

Manifesting works because it involves self-examination and affords your brain the opportunity to update the story of you in ways that more accurately reflect who you really are.

Core Concept: self-knowledge creates a powerful foundation on which to build your future and manifest your dreams. Your sense of self is not immutable, it is simply a story compiled by your brain. You are your brain. You can rewrite the story of you. You are unique. No two manifesting journeys will ever be the same.

CHANGE

Change is an inherent capacity of the human brain. Manifesting is like a training programme for changing your brain. We are how we predictably think, feel and act. These predictable patterns feel like an unchangeable part of who we are. But they are not inherent, they are learned.

It is the human brain's incredible capacity for change that is inherent. Manifesting techniques harness this neuroplasticity to learn new, coherent, focused patterns of thinking, feeling and acting. Manifesting is fundamentally about change. It's about changing your thinking, your behaviour, your reality and your brain.

Core Concept: your brain is built for change but paradoxically your brain resists change. Manifesting works not only because it supports learning harnessing neuroplasticity, but also because it employs techniques that support you through challenge with self-compassion and self-confidence.

CLARITY

Clarity primes your brain to focus attention on what will take you closer to your goal. Visualisation is a really effective manifesting technique to gain clarity about what you really want. With clarity, your brain can filter out the unimportant and draw your attention to salient information and opportunities.

By emphasising clarity, manifesting taps into the brain's salience network, filtering incoming information, focusing attention and amplifying the important and relevant, guiding your actions towards achieving your goals. Clarity stems from the foundational manifesting step of self-awareness. Reflecting on who you are, what you enjoy and where your natural abilities lie can help you find flow.

Core Concept: once you have clarity about what you want, focused attention rather than attraction is what drives successful manifesting. What we pay attention to, our beliefs, our values, our prejudices, our culture and life experience don't just affect how we perceive something but whether we perceive something at all. When you experience flow it becomes easier to visualise and manifest your goals. Being fully engaged in what you're doing brings a clarity of purpose that can help make your manifestation more specific and tangible.

COHERENCE

Coherence ensures that your behaviour, including your thinking, emotions and actions, is aligned and connected to your authentic self and the goals that you wish to manifest. Coherence requires self-regulation so that you can take the focused action necessary to bring about the change you desire.

Manifesting is a form of self-regulation that supplements and supports the frontal lobes of your brain to ensure that everything you do, think and feel is aligned and connected to your authentic self and the goals that you wish to manifest. Manifesting offers a good balance between the development of unconscious, positive, goal-oriented habitual behaviours and present-focused, goal-oriented action.

Core Concept: manifesting helps you to make goal-focused behaviour and positive thinking habitual. The repetition and the regularity of practising various manifesting techniques helps you to build unconscious habits that keep you on track, help you avoid the pitfall of procrastination and propel you towards your goals.

CREATE

Create a new reality and a new you. The core manifesting techniques outlined in the final chapter will help you to do just that. When you treat yourself with respect and compassion and connect with your authentic self, visualisation will help you to gain clarity about what you truly want.

Affirmations can help you to attain your manifesting goals by rewiring your thought patterns, nurturing motivation and self-belief while also cultivating a positive outlook. Journaling can help you track progress and better understand yourself and your emotions. Gratitude brings happiness and 'acting as if' and meditation can change your brain.

Core Concept: the manifesting techniques mentioned in this book are grounded in science and beneficial in numerous ways that will not only help you to attain your manifesting goals, but also improve your mental wellbeing, your sense of contentment and happiness as well as your quality of life.

Go now and create your best life. The power to do so lies entirely within you, within your brain. Manifesting works, and now you know how.

Bibliography

Introduction

Curiosity

Aiyana, K.W., Ara, N., (2013). 'Cognitive biases explain religious belief, paranormal belief and belief in life's purpose', *Cognition*, 129, 2, 379–391, DOI: 10.1016/j.cognition.2013.07.016.

Azar, Beth, (2010). 'A reason to believe', *Monitor on Psychology*, Vol 41, No 11.

Boyack, K.W., Klavans, R., and Börner, K., (2005). 'Mapping the backbone of science', *Scientometrics*, *64*, 351–374.

Butler, A.C., Chapman, J.E., Forman, E.M., and Beck, A.T., (2006). 'The empirical status of cognitive-behavioural therapy: a review of meta-analyses', *Clinical Psychology Review*, Vol 26(1), 17–31.

Cuijpers, P., Karyotaki, E., Weitz, E., Andersson, G., Hollon, S.D., and van Straten, A., (2014). 'The effects of psychotherapies for major depression in adults on remission, recovery and improvement: a meta-analysis'. *Journal of Affective Disorders*, 159, 118–126.

Dixon, L.J., Hornsey, M.J., and Hartley, N., (2023). '"The Secret" to Success? The psychology of belief in manifestation', *Personality and Social Psychology Bulletin* 1:17, DOI: 10.1177/01461672231181162

Djulbegovic, B., Hozo, I., Beckstead, J. et al., (2012). 'Dual processing model of medical decision-making', *BMC Med Inform Decis Mak* **12**, 94, DOI: 10.1186/1472-6947-12-94

Editors (2002). 'The peculiar institution'. *Scientific American*, *286*, 8.

Evans, J. St B.T., and Stanovich, K.E., (2013). 'Dual-Process Theories of Higher Cognition: Advancing the Debate', *Perspectives on Psychological Science*, 8(3), 223–241, DOI: 10.1177/1745691612460685

Forer, B.R., (1949). 'The fallacy of personal validation: a classroom demonstration of gullibility', *The Journal of Abnormal and Social Psychology*, 44 (1), 118–123, DOI: 10.1037/h0059240

Frith, C., (2021). 'The neural basis of consciousness', *Psychological Medicine*, 51(4), 550–562, DOI: 10.1017/S0033291719002204

Gecewicz, C., (2017). '"New Age" beliefs common among both religious and non-religious Americans', The Pew Research Center – downloaded 19/1/2023, www.pewrsr.ch/2NR7Bme

Hofmann, S.G., Asnaani, A., Vonk, I.J., Sawyer, A.T., and Fang, A., (2012). 'The Efficacy of Cognitive Behavioural Therapy: A Review of Meta-analyses', *Cognitive Therapy and Research*, 36(5), 427–440, DOI: 10.1007/s10608-012-9476-1

Hofmann, W., Schmeichel, B.J., Baddeley, A.D., (2012). 'Executive functions and self-regulation', *Trends Cognitive Science* Mar;16(3):174–80, DOI: 10.1016/j.tics.2012.01.006. Epub 2012 Feb 13. PMID: 22336729.

Houpt, A., (2021). 'Covid brought "manifestation" back. But you can't simply will your way to a better life', *Washington Post*, www.washingtonpost.com/lifestyle/wellness/manifest-attraction-covid-work-369/2021/03/12/62d22144-81f6-11eb-9ca6-54e187ee4939_story.html

Huang, J., (2019). 'Greater brain activity during the resting state and the control of activation during the performance of tasks', *Sci Rep*, 9, 5027, DOI: 10.1038/s41598-019-41606-2

Hutcherson, C.A., Seppala, E.M., and Gross, J.J., (2008). 'Loving-kindness meditation increases social connectedness', *Emotion*, 8(5), 720–724.

Nafousi, R., (2022). *Manifest – Seven Steps to Living your Best Life*. Penguin.

Nash, K., Kleinert, T., Leota, J., Scott, A., and Schimel, J., (2022). 'Resting-state networks of believers and non-believers: An EEG microstate study', *Biological Psychology*, Vol 169, 108283, DOI: 10.1016/j.biopsycho.2022.108283

National Institute for Health and Care Excellence (2019). 'Depression in adults: recognition and management. Clinical guideline' [CG90] Published: 28/10/2009, www.nice.org.uk/guidance/cg90

National Institute for Health and Care Excellence (2019). 'Generalised anxiety disorder and panic disorder in adults: management. Clinical guideline' [CG113] Published: 26/01/2011, www.nice.org.uk/guidance/cg113

Sambuco, N., Bradley, M.M., and Lang, P.J., (2022). 'Narrative imagery: Emotional modulation in the default mode network', *Neuropsychologia*, Vol 164, DOI: 10.1016/j.neuropsychologia.2021.108087.

Stephens, G.J., Silbert, L.J., and Hasson, U., (2010). 'Speaker–listener neural coupling underlies successful communication', *Proceedings of the National Academy of Sciences of the United States of America*, 107(32), 14425–14430.

Swart, Tara, (2019). *The Source – Open Your Mind, Change your Life*. Vermilion.

Tang, Y., Holzel, B., Posner, M., (2015). 'The Neuroscience of Mindfulness Meditation', *Nature Reviews Neuroscience*, 16 (4) 213–225.

Thibaut, F., (2018). 'The mind–body Cartesian dualism and psychiatry', *Dialogues Clin Neurosci.* Mar;20(1):3., DOI: 10.31887/DCNS.2018.20.1/fthibaut. PMID: 29946205; PMCID: PMC6016047.

Truesdale, Rose, (2021). 'The Manifestation Business Moves Past Positive Thinking and Into Science', www.vice.com. Retrieved 26/03/2023.

Vaccaro, G., Scott, B., Gimbel, S.I., Kaplan, J.T., (2021). 'Functional Brain Connectivity During Narrative Processing Relates to Transportation and Story Influence', Frontiers in Human Neuroscience, Vol 15, DOI: 10.3389/fnhum.2021.665319

de Waal, F., (2009). *The Age of Empathy: Nature's Lessons for a Kinder Society.* Harmony Books.

Part One

Chapter One: Compassion

Allen, M., et al., (2012). 'Cognitive-affective neural plasticity following active controlled mindfulness intervention', *Journal of Neuroscience*, 32 (44): 15601–15610.

Beer, J.S., and Hughes, B.L., (2011). 'Self-enhancement: A social neuroscience perspective' In: Mark, D.A., Constantine, S., eds, *Handbook of Self-Enhancement and Self-Protection*, 1st ed New York: The Guilford Press 49–65.

Brown, K.W., Ryan, R.M., (2003). 'The benefits of being present: Mindfulness and its role in psychological wellbeing', *Journal of Personality and Social Psychology*, 84 (4), 822–848.

Goldsmith-Turro, R., (2022). 'Changing the Habit of Self-Criticism', *Psychology Today.*

Longe, et al., (2010). 'Having a word with yourself: Neural correlated of self-criticism and self-reassurance', *NeuroImage*, 49:1849–1856.

Neff, K., (2021). *Self-Compassion – The Proven Power of Being Kind To Yourself*, Yellow Kite.

Neff, K.D., (2003). 'Self-compassion: An alternative conceptualisation of a healthy attitude toward oneself', *Self and Identity*, 2(2), 85–101.

Stevens, L., and Woodruff, C.C., eds, (2018). *The Neuroscience of Empathy, Compassion and Self-Compassion*, Academic Press, London.

Chapter Two: Connection

Agarwal, Pragya, (2020). *Sway – Unravelling Unconscious Bias*, Bloomsbury Sigma.

Budaev, S., Jorgensen, C., Mangel, M., Eliassen, S., and Giske, J., (2019). 'Decision-making from the Animal Perspective: Bridging Ecology and Subjective Cognition', *Frontiers in Ecology and Evolution*, Vol 7, DOI: 10.3389/fevo/2019.00164

Dickerson, B.C., and Eichenbaum, H., (2010). 'The episodic memory system: neurocircuitry and disorders', *Neuropsychopharmacology*, 35, 86–104, DOI: 10.1038/npp.2009.126

Eagleman, D., (2014). *The Brain – The Story of You*, Canongate Books.

Eagleman, D., (2020). *Livewired – The Inside Story of the Ever-Changing Brain*, Canongate Books.

Feldman Barret, L., (2021). 'This is how your brain makes your mind', *MIT Technology Review – Biotechnology*. Retrieved 3/4/2023, www.technologyreview.com/2021/08/25/1031432

Hay, L., (1984). *You Can Heal Your Life*, Hay House.

Hickman, L., (2014). *The Nature of the Self and the Contemplation of Nature: Ecotheology and the History of the Soul in the Concept of the Soul: Scientific and Religious Perspectives*. Fuller, M., (ed.). Cambridge Scholars Publishing.

Jang, K.L., Livesley, W.J., and Vernon, P.A., (1996). 'Heritability of the big five personality dimensions and their facets: a twin study', *Journal of Personality*, 64(3), 577–591.

Khanna, A., Pascual-Leone, A., Michel, C.M., Farzan, F., (2015). 'Microstates in resting-state EEG: current status and future directions', *Neurosci Biobehav Rev.*, Feb; 49:105–13, DOI: 10.1016/j.neubiorev.2014.12.010

Klussman, K., Curtin, N., Langer, J., and Lee Nichols, A., (2022). 'The Importance of Awareness, Acceptance and Alignment with the Self: A Framework for Understanding Self-Connection', *Europe's Journal of Psychology*, Vol 18, (1), 120–131, DOI: 10.5964/ejop.3707

Lage, C.A., Wolmarans, D.W., and Mograbi, D.C., (2022). 'An Evolutionary View of Self-Awareness'. *Behavioural Processes*, 1, DOI: 10.1016/j.bproc.2021.104543

LeDoux, J.E., Michel, M., and Lau, H., (2020). Edited by Ungerleider L.G., 'A little history goes a long way towards understanding why we study consciousness the way we do today.' *PNAS*, 117 (13) 6976-6984, DOI: 10.1073/pnas.1921623117

Loftus, E., (2018). 'How memory can be manipulated', *Speaking of Psychology Podcast*, Ep 91, www.apa.org/news/podcasts/speaking-of-psychology/memory-manipulated. Transcript retrieved 11/4/2023.

Loftus, E., (2013). 'How reliable is your memory?' [Video]. TEDGlobal – TED Conferences, www.ted.com/talks/elizabeth_loftus_how_reliable_is_your_memory/transcript

Lou, H.C., Changeux, A.R., (2017). 'Towards a cognitive neuroscience of self-awareness', *Neuroscience and Behavioural Reviews*, Vol 83, Pages 765–773.

Mehta, N., (2011). 'Mind–body Dualism: A Critique from a Health Perspective', *Brain, Mind and Consciousness: An International, Interdisciplinary Perspective* (A.R. Singh and S.A. Singh, eds.), MSM, 9(1), pp 202–209.

Mitchell, K., (2018). *Innate: How the Wiring of Our Brains Shapes Who We Are*, Princeton University Press.

Nagel, Thomas, (1974). 'What Is It Like to Be a Bat?'. *The Philosophical Review*, 83 (4): 435–450, DOI: 10.2307/2183914. JSTOR 2183914.

Nani, A., Manuello, J., Mancuso, L., Liloia, D., Costa, T., and Cauda, F., (2019). 'The neural correlates of consciousness and attention: two sister processes of the brain', *Frontiers in Neuroscience*, 13: 1169, DOI: 10.3389/fnins.2019.01169

Owen, A., (2017). *Into the Grey Zone – A Neuroscientist Explores the Border Between Life and Death*, Guardian Faber Publishing.

Roediger, H.L. III, and Marsh, E.J., (2003). 'Episodic and Autobiographical Memory Part Six', *Handbook of Psychology*, I.B. Weiner (ed.), DOI: 10.1002/0471264385. wei0417

Seth, A., (2022). *Being You – The New Science of Consciousness*, Faber and Faber.

Stallen, M., and Sanfrey, A.G., (2015). 'The neuroscience of social conformity: implications for fundamental and applied research', *Frontiers in Neuroscience*, 9, DOI: 10.3389/fnins.2015.00337

Part Two

Chapter Three: Change

Bos, M.W., Dijksterhuis, A., and van Baaren, R., (2012). 'Food for thought? Trust your unconscious when energy is low', *Journal of Neuroscience, Psychology, and Economics, 5*(2), 124–130, DOI: 10.1037/a0027388

Clark, A., (2013). 'Whatever next? Predictive brains, situated agents, and the future of cognitive science', *Behavioural and Brain Sciences*, 36(3), 181–204, www.cambridge.org/core/journals/behavioral-and-brain-sciences/article/whatever-next-predictive-brains-situated-agents-and-the-future-of-cognitive-science/33542 C736E17E3D1D44E8D03BE5F4CD9

Eggermont, J.J., (2017). 'Multisensory processing', *Hearing Loss.*

Friston, K., (2010). 'The free-energy principle: a unified brain theory?' *Nature Reviews Neuroscience*, 11(2), 127–138, www.nature.com/articles/nrn2787

Friston, K., and Kiebel, S., (2009). 'Predictive coding under the free-energy principle', *Philosophical Transactions of the Royal Society B: Biological Sciences*, 364(1521), 1211–1221, DOI: 10.1098/rstb.2008.0300

Gardner, B., (2012). 'Busting the 21-day habit formation myth', *Health Chatter: Research Department of Behavioural Science Blog*, University College London. Retrieved 18/04/2023, www.blogs.ucl.ac.uk/bsh/2012/06/29/busting-the-21-days-habit-formation-myth

Lewton, Thomas, (2021). 'Is reality real?', *New Scientist*, 252(3359):38–41.

Milkman, Katy, (2021), *How to Change – The Science of Getting to Where You Want to Be.* Vermilion.

Public Domain, www.commons.wikimedia.org/w/index.php?curid=667017. Retrieved 27/01/23. Original Source: Jastrow, J., (1899). 'The mind's eye', *Popular Science Monthly*, **54**, 299–312.

Raichle, M.E., and Gusnard, D.A., (2002). 'Appraising the brain's energy budget' 99 (16) 10237–10239, DOI: 10.1073/pnas.172399499

Ryrie, A., (2010). https://blog.oup.com/2010/09/magic

Seth, Anil, (2022). *Being You – The New Science of Consciousness.* Faber and Faber.

Shinohara, Ryuu, (2019). *The Magic of Manifesting – 15 Advanced Techniques to Attract your Best Life, Even if you Think it's Impossible Now.* Independently published.

Sinclair, A.H., Manalili, G.M., Brunec, I.K., Adcock, R.A., and Barense, M.D., (2021). 'Prediction errors disrupt hippocampal representations and update episodic memory', *PNAS*, 118 (51) e2117625118, DOI: 10.1073/pnas.2117625118

Steffan, P.R., Hedges, D., and Matheson, R., (2022). 'The brain is adaptive not triune: how the brain responds to threat, challenge and change', *Front. Psychiatry*, Vol 13 – 2022, DOI: 10.3389/fpsyt.2022.802606

Teufel, C., Dakin, S.C. and Fletcher, P.C., (2018). 'Prior object-knowledge sharpens properties of early visual feature-detectors', *Sci Rep*, 8, 10853, DOI: 10.1038/s41598-018-28845-5

Verplanken, B., and Sui J., (2019). 'Habit and Identity: Behavioural, Cognitive, Affective and Motivational Facets of Integrated Self', *Frontiers in Psychology*, Vol 10, DOI: 10/fpsyg.2019.01504

Chapter Four: Clarity

Csikszentmihalyi, M., (1990). *Flow: The Psychology of Optimal Experience*, Harper & Row.

Dietrich, A., (2004). 'Neurocognitive mechanisms underlying the experience of flow', *Consciousness and Cognition*, 13(4), 746–761.

Eichenbaum, H., (2017). 'On the Integration of Space, Time, and Memory', *Neuron*, 95(5), 1007–1018.

Fredrickson, B.L., (2001). 'The Role of Positive Emotions in Positive Psychology: The Broaden-and-Build Theory of Positive Emotions', *American Psychologist,* 56(3), 218–226.

Fuster, J.M., (2001). 'The prefrontal cortex – an update: time is of the essence', *Neuron*, 30(2), 319–333.

Harris, D.J., Vine, S.J., Wilson, M.R., and Brewer, J., (2017). 'Neurocognitive Mechanisms of the Flow State', *Progress in Brain Research*, 234, 221–243.

Howard-Jones, P.A., (2018). 'Evolution of the brain and intelligence in primates', *Progress in Brain Research*, 236, 1–31.

Locke, E.A., and Latham, G.P., (2006). 'New Directions in Goal-Setting Theory', Current *Directions in Psychological Science*, 15(5), 265–268.

Menon, V., (2015). 'Salience Network', *Brain Mapping: An Encyclopaedic Reference*, Vol 2, pp 597–611, DOI: 10.1016/B978-0-12-397025-1.00052-X

Sheldon, K.M., and Elliot, A.J., (1999). 'Goal Striving, Need Satisfaction and Longitudinal Well-Being: The Self-Concordance Model', *Journal of Personality and Social Psychology*, 76(3), 482–497.

Ulrich, M., Keller, J., and Grön, G., (2016). 'Neural signatures of experimentally induced flow experiences identified in a typical fMRI block design with BOLD imaging', *Social Cognitive and Affective Neuroscience*, 11(3), 496–507.

Wise, R.A., (2004). 'Dopamine, learning and motivation', *Nature Reviews Neuroscience*, 5(6), 483–494.

Yin, H.H., and Knowlton, B.J., (2006). 'The role of the basal ganglia in habit formation', *Nature Reviews Neuroscience*, 7(6), 464–476.

Chapter Five: Coherence

Andreou, C., and White, N.D., eds., (2010). *The Thief of Time: Philosophical Essays on Procrastination*, Oxford University Press.

Bongers, C.A., and Dijksterhuis, A., (2009). 'Unconscious goals and motivation', *Encyclopaedia of Consciousness*, 423–433.

Danner, D.D., Snowdon, D.A., and Friesen, W.V., (2001). 'Positive emotions in early life and longevity: findings from the nun study', *Journal of Personality and Social Psychology*, 80(5), 804–813, www.pubmed.ncbi.nlm.nih.gov/11374751/

Davidson, R.J., and McEwen, B.S., (2012). 'Social influences on neuroplasticity: stress and interventions to promote well-being', *Nature Neuroscience*, 15(5), 689–695, www.nature.com/articles/nn.3093

Fredrickson, B.L., et al., (2008). 'Open hearts build lives: positive emotions, induced through loving-kindness meditation, build consequential personal resources', *Journal of Personality and Social Psychology*, 95(5), 1045–1062, www.pubmed.ncbi.nlm.nih.gov/18954193/

Gustavson, D.E., Miyake, A., Hewitt, J.K., and Friedman, N.P., (2014). 'Genetic relations among procrastination, impulsivity and goal management ability: Implications for the evolutionary origin of procrastination', *Psychological Science*, 25 (6), DOI: 10.1177/0956797614526260

Klingberg, T., (2010). 'Training and plasticity of working memory', *Trends Cogn. Sci.*, 14, 317–324.

Robinson, H., et al., (2014). 'Neuroanatomical correlates of executive functions: A neuropsychological approach using the EXAMINER battery', *J Int Neuropsychol Soc.* 2014 Jan; 20(1): 52–63.

Surowiecki, J., (2010). 'Later: What does procrastination tell us about ourselves?' *The New Yorker.*

Zhang, S., Liu, P., Feng, T., (2018). 'To do it now or later: The cognitive mechanisms and neural substrates underlying procrastination', *WIREs: Cognitive Science*, DOI: 10.1002/wcs.1492

Chapter Six: Create

Arora, S., et al., (2011). 'Mental practice enhances surgical technical skills: a randomized controlled study', *Annals of Surgery*, 253(2), 265–270.

Bem, D.J., (1972). 'Self-perception theory', *Advances in Experimental Social Psychology*, Vol 6, pp 1–62, Academic Press, www.sciencedirect.com/science/article/pii/S0065260108600289

Braver, S.L., et al., (2014). 'Mechanisms of Self-Control in Adolescents and Adults: Adaptive Changes in Mental Representations and Physiological Responses', *Psychological Science*, 25(11), 2065–2073, www.ncbi.nlm.nih.gov/pubmed/25213456

Critcher, C.R., and Dunning, D., (2015). 'Self-affirmations provide a broader perspective on self-threat', *Personality and Social Psychology Bulletin*, 41(1), 3–18, DOI: 10.1177/0146167214554956

DeSteno, D., Gross, J.J., and Kubzansky, L., (2013). 'Affective science and health: The importance of emotion and emotion regulation', *Health Psychology*, 32(5), 474–486, www.ncbi.nlm.nih.gov/pmc/articles/PMC3751086

Driskell, J.E., Copper, C., and Moran, A., (1994). 'Does mental practice enhance performance?' *Journal of Applied Psychology*, 79(4), 481–492.

Dweck, C., (2008). *Mindset: The New Psychology of Success*, Random House, www.worldcat.org/title/mindset-the-new-psychology-of-success/oclc/70671780

Emmons, R.A., and McCullough, M.E., (2003). 'Counting blessings versus burdens: an experimental investigation of gratitude and subjective well-being in daily life', *Journal of Personality and Social Psychology*, 84(2), 377–389, DOI: 10.1037/0022-3514.84.2.377

Fors, E.A., Sexton, H., and Götestam, K.G., (2002). 'The effect of guided imagery and amitriptyline on daily fibromyalgia pain: A prospective, randomized, controlled trial', *Journal of Psychiatric Research*, 36(3), 179–187.

Goyal, M., Singh, S., Sibinga, E.M., Gould, N.F., Rowland-Seymour, A., Sharma, R., and Ranasinghe, P.D., (2014). 'Meditation programs for psychological stress and well-being: a systematic review and meta-analysis', *JAMA Internal Medicine*, 174(3), 357–368, www.jamanetwork.com/journals/jamainternalmedicine/fullarticle/1809754

Hannula, D.E., Ranganath, A., (2008). 'Medial temporal lobe activity predicts successful relational memory binding', *Journal of Neuroscience*, 28(1), 116–124.

Holmes, E.A., and Mathews, A., (2010). 'Mental imagery in emotion and emotional disorders', *Clinical Psychology Review*, 30(3), 349–362. www.pubmed.ncbi.nlm.nih. gov/20170929

Hölzel, B.K., Carmody, J., Vangel, M., et al., (2011). 'Mindfulness practice leads to increases in regional brain grey matter density', *Psychiatry Research: Neuroimaging*, 191(1), 36–43, www.ncbi.nlm.nih.gov/pmc/articles/PMC3004979

Iacoboni, M., et al., (1999). 'Cortical Mechanisms of Human Imitation', *Science*, 286(5449), 2526–2528, www.ncbi.nlm.nih.gov/pubmed/10617472

Jackowska, M., Brown, J., Ronaldson, A., and Steptoe, A., (2016). 'The impact of a brief gratitude intervention on subjective well-being, biology and sleep', *Journal of Health Psychology*, 21(10), 2207–2217.

Kosslyn, S.M., Ganis, G., and Thompson, W.L., (2001). 'Neural foundations of imagery', *Nature Reviews Neuroscience*, 2(9), 635–642, www.nature.com/ articles/35090055

Levenson, R.W., et al., (1992). 'Voluntary Facial Action Generates Emotion-Specific Autonomic Nervous System Activity', *Psychophysiology*, 27(4), 363–384, www.ncbi. nlm.nih.gov/pubmed/1619068

Linden, D.E., (2006). 'How psychotherapy changes the brain – the contribution of functional neuroimaging', *Molecular Psychiatry*, 11(6), 528–538.

Mills, P.J., et al., (2015). 'The Role of Gratitude in Spiritual Well-being in Asymptomatic Heart Failure Patients', *Spirituality in Clinical Practice* (Washington, D.C.), 2(1), 5–17.

Pennebaker, J.W., and Beall, S.K., (1986). 'Confronting a traumatic event: Toward an understanding of inhibition and disease', *Journal of Abnormal Psychology*, 95(3), 274–281, www.pubmed.ncbi.nlm.nih.gov/3745651

Sherman, D.K., and Cohen, G.L., (2006). 'The psychology of self-defence: Self-affirmation theory', *Advances in Experimental Social Psychology*, 38, 183–242, www.sciencedirect.com/science/article/pii/S0065260106380045

Tang, Y.Y., Hölzel, B.K., and Posner, M.I., (2015). 'The neuroscience of mindfulness meditation', *Nature Reviews Neuroscience*, 16(4), 213–225, www.nature.com/ articles/nrn3916

Ullrich, P.M., and Lutgendorf, S.K., (2002). 'Journaling about stressful events: effects of cognitive processing and emotional expression', *Annals of Behavioural Medicine*, 24(3), 244–250, www.pubmed.ncbi.nlm.nih.gov/12173686

Zahn, R., Moll, J., Paiva, M., Garrido, G., Krueger, F., Huey, E.D., and Grafman, J., (2009). 'The Neural Basis of Human Social Values: Evidence from Functional MRI', *Cerebral Cortex*, 19(2), 276–283.

Notes

i   **fMRI** – An MRI scanner uses magnetic fields to create 3D images of the internal
    structures of the body, including the brain. Using the same scanner, scientists can
    also look at brain functioning by tracking changes in blood flow to the brain; this
    is known as fMRI scanning. When an individual is given a task such as remem-
    bering a list of words while in an MRI scanner, the neurons in their brain involved
    in remembering the words become more active than brain cells not involved in
    remembering the list. This neural activity, which takes the form of electrical and
    chemical signals, requires energy. Neurons generate energy by using oxygen to
    break down glucose (aka sugar). The energy used up by increased neural activity
    in the particular part of the brain involved in the task needs to be replenished. As
    supplies diminish more oxygen-carrying blood is transported to the specific part
    of the brain to replenish the energy used. The blood deploys a molecule called
    haemoglobin to transport oxygen to the brain. Haemoglobin contains iron, which
    has magnetic properties.

    The magnetic properties of blood change depending on whether it has oxygen
    (oxygenated) or not (deoxygenated). Brain regions that are more active during the
    task in the scanner are slightly more magnetic than brain areas not directly involved
    in the task. This gives rise to slightly different patterns of electromagnetic waves.
    Essentially fMRI measures brain activity by detecting changes in the amount of
    oxygen in the blood and the amount of blood flow. This measurement, called
    blood-oxygenated-level-dependent activity (BOLD), is a useful proxy measure for
    brain activity.

ii **DNA** – the molecule inside cells that contains the genetic information responsible
    for the development and function of an organism. DNA molecules allow genetic
    information to pass from one generation to the next.

iii **Monozygotic twins** – also known as identical twins, occur when a fertilised egg
    divides in two; each half then develops into two babies each of whom have the
    same genetic information. The twins will be the same sex. About one quarter
    of identical twins are mirror images of each other, with the right side of one twin
    matching the left side of their twin.

iv   **Interactionism** – The position that mind and body are distinct, incompatible sub-
     stances that nevertheless interact, so that each has a causal influence on the other.
     (APA Dictionary dictionary.apap.org – retrieved 3/4/2023)
         This position is particularly associated with René Descartes and his position,
     known as Cartesian dualism. He proposed that the world comprises two distinct
     and incompatible classes of substance: the physical realm of matter (*res extensa*)
     and the mental realm (*res cogitans*). For Descartes, the mind would continue to
     exist even if the material body did not.

v   **Parallelism** – The philosophical proposition that, although mind and body con-
     stitute separate realities, they function in parallel such that their responses seem
     holistic and the two realms seem to assert causal control over each other. (APA
     Dictionary dictionary.apap.org – retrieved 3/4/2023)

vi   **Idealism** – The philosophical position that reality, including the natural world, is
     not independent of mind. Positions range from strong forms, holding that mind
     constitutes the things of reality, to weaker forms, holding that reality is correlated
     with the workings of the mind. There is also a range of positions as to the nature
     of mind, from those holding that mind must be conceived of as absolute, universal
     and apart from nature itself, to those holding that mind may be conceived of as
     individual minds. (APA Dictionary dictionary.apap.org – retrieved 3/4/2023)

vii **Double Aspect Theory** – The philosophical position that mind and body are two
     attributes of a single substance (see mind–body problem). This view is particularly
     associated with Baruch Spinoza, who held that there is one (and only one) infinite
     substance, which he identified as God. (APA Dictionary dictionary.apap.org – re-
     trieved 3/4/2023)

viii **Epiphenomenalism** – The philosophical position that bodily (physical) events
     produce mental events, such as thoughts and feelings, but that mental events do
     not have causal power to produce bodily (physical) events. Thus, causality between
     the mental and the physical proceeds in one direction only. A more radical form of
     the same position would add that mental events lack causal efficacy to produce
     anything, including other mental events.

ix   **Materialism** – The philosophical position that everything, including mental events,
     is composed of physical matter and is thus subject to the laws of physics. From
     this perspective, the mind is considered to exist solely as a set of brain processes.

Acknowledgements

Jane Graham Maw, without you this book would not exist. Thank you for nudging me in the best direction. You are an amazing agent, I am so fortunate to be one of your authors.

Pippa, thank you for believing in and fighting for this book in the face of competition. I wish you continued success and happiness. Every author hopes for an insightful editor; I feel doubly blessed to have two. Pippa Wright and Jessica Duffy you are both brilliant, thank you for your insightful edits. Jessica, it's been really lovely working with you, and I look forward to the rest of our publishing journey together.

Every garden requires a gardener, and our eight-acre garden demands more than one. As I wrote this book, the garden constantly called to me through every window for care and attention. Having read this book you will know that gardening is my go-to procrastination activity, but had I succumbed every day there would be no book. Nonetheless, I couldn't bear to see it suffer while I wrote so I am especially grateful to Emma, Glynn, William, Kathleen, Christine, Debbi, Karoline, Catherine, Nathan, Sigi and Jack for the amazing work you did tending to the garden when I could not – it is looking splendid as I write these words.

Marianne Power, thank you for allowing me to tell your money story and for writing *Help Me!*. I can't wait to read your next book, *Love Me!*.

Dr Amanda Darnley, Caroline Labouchere and Glyniss Trinder – a huge thanks to each of you for taking the time to speak with me and for sharing your personal and professional insights on manifesting.

Finally, and most importantly, to my best friend, my husband David – thank you for your kindness and understanding. You are simply the best.

Credits

Orion Spring would like to thank everyone at Orion who worked on the publication of *The Neuroscience of Manifesting*.

Agent
Jane Graham Maw

Editor
Jessica Duffy

Editorial Management
Georgia Goodall
Carina Bryan
Jane Hughes
Charlie Panayiotou
Lucy Bilton
Claire Boyle

Copy-editor
Joanne Gledhill

Proofreader
Jacqui Lewis

Audio
Paul Stark
Jake Alderson
Georgina Cutler

Contracts
Dan Herron
Ellie Bowker
Alyx Hurst

Design
Nick Shah

Jessica Hart

Joanna Ridley

Helen Ewing

Photo Shoots & Image Research
Natalie Dawkins

Finance
Nick Gibson

Jasdip Nandra

Sue Baker

Tom Costello

Inventory
Jo Jacobs

Dan Stevens

Operations
Group Sales Operations team

Rights
Rebecca Folland

Tara Hiatt

Ben Fowler

Alice Cottrell

Ruth Blakemore

Marie Henckel

Production
Hannah Cox

Katie Horrocks

Marketing
Javerya Iqbal

Publicity
Elizabeth Allen

Sales
Jen Wilson

Victoria Laws

Esther Waters

Tolu Ayo-Ajala

Group Sales teams across
        Digital, Field, International
        and Non-Trade

About the Author

Dr Sabina Brennan is a chartered health psychologist, neuroscientist, award-winning science communicator, author of the international bestsellers *100 Days to a Younger Brain* and *Beating Brain Fog,* and host of the critically acclaimed *Super Brain* podcast.

Dr Brennan was a principal investigator on multiple brain health research projects at Trinity College Dublin, where she was also director of the Neuro-Enhancement for Independent Lives dementia research programme. Dr Brennan now specialises in translating complex neuroscience into easy to understand, practical information for broadcast media and wellness talks.

Dr Brennan has been engaged as an advisor to governments and global businesses influencing policy and practice in the areas of brain health, ageing, dementia, migraine and multiple sclerosis. She also volunteers on scientific advisory boards and advocacy panels supporting charities, non-profits and NGOs.